PASTORAL PROBLEMS in FIRST CORINTHIANS

PASTORAL PROBLEMS in FIRST CORINTHIANS

by
J. STANLEY GLEN

The Epworth Press
LONDON

PRINTED AND BOUND IN ENGLAND BY
HAZELL WATSON AND VINEY LTD
AYLESBURY, BUCKS

CONTENTS

FOREWORD

This interpretation of The First Letter of Paul to the Corinthians arose out of the rather unusual circumstance of having to teach in two different fields of theological study at the same time. The responsibility of providing a course in pastoral theology concurrently with a major responsibility in New Testament over a period of years led to a certain integration of the two fields. The artificial distinction which would consider the one practical and the other theoretical tended to disappear. This was particularly the case with the present letter. The pastoral orientation enabled one to see that it had a greater relevance to the life and work of the contemporary modern church than could have been recognized from a strictly objective, academic approach. Encouragement in this direction came from students, ministers, and missionaries on furlough who indicated the relevance of the letter to their own experience.

There is always a risk, however, in such a venture. To relax the strict objectivity of textual study in order to see those relationships between the Bible and contemporary life which make for relevance increases the possibility of error. A proper balance between objectivity and an intuitive participation in real life is therefore necessary. In a certain important respect, objectivity and relevance are mutually exclusive, just as in another respect they are complementary. Such a risk is greater in some sections of the letter than in others, particularly in

7

those which involve controversial issues. Since the interpretation in certain instances cuts across accepted and conventional views of what the letter is saying, it may prompt the accusation that extraneous meanings have been put into it. The writer has decided to accept this risk because it seems the inevitable price of any attempt at relevant interpretation. In any event the stimulation of a greater appreciation of the pastoral significance of the letter will be a sufficient reward despite the limitations that may qualify the effort.

The arrangement of subject matter follows the same order as the material in the letter. In this respect it resembles a commentary. But the purpose is essentially thematic. This will become apparent as the reader considers not only the theme of each section but the manner in which certain themes thread their way through the whole letter. The number of references cited may seem larger than necessary, but they have been given to indicate the background of material from which the study has emerged. Their inclusion has seemed especially important since exegetical detail has been kept to a minimum.

Sincere gratitude is expressed to the staff of The Westminster Press for a number of helpful suggestions respecting literary style. Their interest and encouragement has always been much appreciated.

J. S. G.

I

INTRODUCTION

The First Letter to the Corinthians is one of the best sources of knowledge of early Christian pastoral care. Although not ordinarily considered a pastoral letter, it probably has a greater claim to this distinction than any other letter. Addressed to a church situated in one of the most profligate cities of the Roman Empire, it portrays the deep, uncompromising struggle of a pastor for the salvation of his people. He bears them upon his soul with a love that cannot abandon them to the power and subtlety of the peculiar temptations to which they were susceptible. As those who had only recently heard the gospel, they could not leave all their past behind or resist the infiltration of all that was contrary to their faith. Even the most devout could not escape some effects of the notorious diversity of superstition, sophistry, and religion for which their cosmopolitan seaport city was well known. They were not wholly immune to its moral and spiritual confusion and its opportunism.

It is evident that a large proportion of the people of the Corinthian church were problem characters who disrupted its fellowship and confronted Paul with a greater variety of difficulty than he had probably experienced in any other church. The list resembles a succession of case studies: dissensions, lawsuits, immorality, broken marriages, divided attitudes toward paganism, serious disorders of worship, and false conceptions of destiny. The rough, low-class constituency from which he recruited most of its members undoubtedly contributed to these difficulties, even though his accomplishment testified to the vigor of his evangelism. Yet out of his experience with such people much was said and written of lasting significance. The variety of the problems and pastoral directives are of surprising relevance to the life and work of the average modern congregation. While there are two extremes to be avoided — that of finding in the Corinthian church the identical problems of the modern church, and that of finding in it only what is so exceptional that it has no relevance to the modern church — there are significant parallels that qualify the letter as one of the best sources of pastoral theology for contemporary use. With the increasingly cosmopolitan and urban population of the modern world, its rapid social change, its mixing and blending of races, nationalities, and religions, and its confused moral and spiritual standards, a situation has emerged which has certain affinities with ancient Corinth. Although the inevitable differences between the ancient past and the modern present will always remain, these seem less significant than the similarities, particularly when it is a question of the extremity of the problems that break through to the surface. Despite the impression of order, success, and goodwill in an average congregation, there are undercurrents and peculiar complexes of mind and spirit that emerge with surprisingly little provocation. What breaks through to the surface in the privacy of a confession or in a critical situation is just as extreme as anything recorded in the letter.

An outline of the specific problems of the letter will suggest their relevance to the modern church. The initial concern is with various dissensions in the congregation that have arisen over competing loyalties to ministers (chs. 1:10 to 4:21). These implicitly idolatrous attachments to men are evidence of a failure to understand the gospel as mature believers. The people hear the word of their favorite man as an expression of his religion, and not as the revelation of the living, contemporaneous Christ. This is the problem of ecumenicity in a pastoral context.

In the two major problems of discipline that follow (chs. 5:1 to 6:11) we have an illustration of the extremes to which Christian people will go when their conduct is not restrained by the ethical sensitivity associated with maturity of faith. In the one instance the congregation is complacent toward a prominent member guilty of incest, and fail to deal with him. In the other instance they display a strange readiness to go to law against one another over relatively trivial matters. Their complacency on the one hand and their precipitousness on the other are opposite phases of their inability to discipline themselves.

In the midsection of the letter (chs. 6:12 to 7:40) two opposite types of sexual problems emerge. There is a libertinism that condones immoral relations with prostitutes as an expression of Christian freedom. And there is an asceticism that so emphasizes sexual abstinence that it disrupts the normal relations of marital life. In neither instance is there any recognition of the incompatibility of the conduct with the Christian faith. Whether free expression or loveless purity, there is no awareness of how each contradicts devotion to Christ.

These two opposite attitudes to sex, which in various degrees are so often associated with religion no less in the modern than in the ancient world, anticipate the theme of the subsequent section (chs. 8:1 to 10:33). This concerns the nature and limits of Christian freedom. The immediate issue is that of eating meat consecrated to idols, with some persons refraining from all meat and others irresponsibly tolerant even to the point of attending feasts in pagan temples. If we recognize that the meat is only incidental to the problem of freedom, we will see that the real issue concerns the extent to which a believer may involve himself in pagan (or secular) practices without compromising his faith.

A series of problems follow (chs. 11:1 to 14:40) that may be generally classified as disorders of worship. These illustrate the extent to which the worship of the church has been confused by tendencies similar to those which have disrupted its total life. There is an assertion of feminine freedom; profanation of the Lord's Supper; rivalry over spiritual gifts, services, and accomplishments; and a strong emphasis on speaking in ecstatic tongues. As Paul analyzes these problems, he sees that they are all indicative of a lack of that unique love of which Christ himself is definitive, namely, agape. This is the love which is revealed not only in the cross but in the resurrection of Christ from the dead. The implication is that all the previous problems are indicative of the same deficiency of love.

In the concluding section (ch. 15:1-58), apart from the final chapter on personal matters, the focus of attention is on the problem of destiny. As it relates to practical life, it concerns the question of ultimate motivation — the change that the gospel brings in the goals for which men strive. In this respect the Corinthians had failed to recognize that the resurrection of Christ was the promise of their resurrection. They had not realized how he had defined their destiny. This failure was implicit in the previous problems of the letter insofar as they presupposed a perspective on life devoid of such a hope.

Paul's approach to such a variety of problems was not that of a perfectionist who expected all serious difficulties of doctrine and of personal life to disappear with the acceptance of Jesus as Lord. The significant fact is that he does not attempt to evangelize the congregation in revivalistic style as if the problems were the result of a failure of previous attempts to evangelize or of a lapse into unbelief. Nor does he summon an evangelist in his absence who will arouse the people to a more vigorous expression of faith. Instead he recognizes the fact that they have heard the gospel and believed. He considers them babes in Christ who need a pastor rather than an evangelist. They require wise counsel and instruction that will minister to their maturity. Although he is firm and uncompromising and frank to the point of severity, he is patient and restrained. His fundamental attitude is illustrated by the fact that he addresses the Corinthians as those who are consecrated and called to be saints (ch. 1:2) and who are his beloved children begotten through the gospel (ch. 4:15).

As a counselor he appeals not to their wisdom but to their

faith in Christ. Instead of throwing them back upon themselves as if to find ultimate answers from within, he throws them back upon the Crucified One. This is a reliance not upon one who is merely dead and buried and therefore of the past but upon one who is risen and contemporaneous. Consequently the answers to their problems are Christological interpretations with a personal orientation. In the context of the difficulties to which the answers correspond, each is a communication of the gospel. In one way or another each is concerned with that freedom from guilt and a death-conditioned existence which comes only through the forgiveness of sins. The hope of the resurrection of the dead is the ultimate, objectified form of forgiveness for the whole man. In this hope Paul sees the individual not as an independent, isolated being but as a member of the covenanted community. Neither the individual nor the community are ends in themselves but are part of that cosmic whole which the redemptive purpose of God comprehends. The pastoral task is understood within this eschatological perspective. If the expression may be permitted, it is practical eschatology.

II

IDOLATROUS LOYALTIES
TO RELIGIOUS LEADERS
1:1-3, 10-17

1 *Paul, called by the will of God to be an apostle of Christ Jesus, and our brother Sosthenes,*

2 *To the church of God which is at Corinth, to those sanctified in Christ Jesus, called to be saints together with all those who in every place call on the name of our Lord Jesus Christ, both their Lord and ours:*

3 *Grace to you and peace from God our Father and the Lord Jesus Christ.*

10 *I appeal to you, brethren, by the name of our Lord Jesus Christ, that all of you agree and that there be no dissensions among you, but that you be united in the same mind and the same judgment.* [11] *For it has been reported to me by Chloe's people that there is quarreling among you, my brethren.* [12] *What I mean is that each one of you says, "I belong to Paul," or "I belong to Apollos," or "I belong to Cephas," or "I belong to Christ."* [13] *Is Christ divided? Was Paul crucified for you? Or were you baptized in the name of Paul?* [14] *I am thankful that I baptized none of you except Crispus and Gaius;* [15] *lest any one should say that you were baptized in my name.* [16] *(I did baptize also the household of Stephanas. Beyond that, I do not know whether I baptized any one else.)* [17] *For Christ did not send me to baptize but to preach the gospel, and not with eloquent wisdom, lest the cross of Christ be emptied of its power.*

It is always a serious problem for the church when its people are attracted more to ministers than to Christ and when as a consequence its ministers tend to become competitors of Christ. For no matter whether this unfortunate state of affairs is encouraged by ministers or by the people, or whether it is a mutual consolidation of a relationship that prevents both from hearing the gospel, it is implicitly idolatrous. This will explain why, as one of the problems that confronted Paul in the Corinthian church, it received his immediate attention in advance of other problems that were undoubtedly communicated to him. It constituted a dangerous internal threat to the church and its faith.

The evidence is sufficiently clear to give us a general appreciation of the circumstances. The people were taking the initiative in promoting the apostle whose spiritual significance had impressed them most and who for this reason they exalted at the expense of their faith in Christ. Some were for Paul, some for Apollos, some for Cephas, and some for Christ, who in this instance was the object of a party loyalty and whose identity has been the subject of perennial speculation. The divided loyalties which in this manner involved the several apostles who had labored among them were the cause of serious dissension in the church as each group played the man of its choice against the others in a spirit of rivalry. Although a form of unity prevailed, as we see from the fact that the groups still worshiped together, it was under serious strain, and quarrels were breaking out. Consequently, there was an urgent need for the kind of action that Paul was quick to provide, both in dispatching his letter and in the plea for harmony which it contained.

"I appeal to you, brethren, by the name of our Lord Jesus Christ, that all of you agree and that there be no dissensions among you, but that you be united in the same mind and the same judgment. For it has been reported to me by Chloe's people that there is quarreling among you, my brethren. What I mean is that each of you says, ' I belong to Paul,' or ' I belong to Apollos,' or ' I belong to Cephas ' or ' I belong to Christ.' " (Ch. 1:10-12.)

The resemblance this problem bears to that so often observed in the long history of the church at any ecclesiastical level will be fairly evident. Loyalties to those who for various reasons have acquired spiritual significance in the lives of others tend to create the kind of confidence in men that is incompatible with faith in Christ. These loyalties, of course, are not unrelated to the general category of hero worship, and in recent times to its modern equivalent, the cult of personality. But their closest connection is with those loyalties which have a basis of intimacy and which readily become idolatrous, as illustrated by the warning of Christ, " He who loves father or mother more than me is not worthy of me " (Matt. 10:37). The name of a reformer, theologian, bishop, evangelist, teacher, or healer may easily become the object of doubtful enthusiasm, and a wide constituency of disciples may appear. Or a preacher, pastor, church official, or patron may acquire popularity and surround himself with a coterie of friends and followers, often for reasons surprisingly unrelated to the faith formally professed.

The variety of factors responsible for these loyalties as well as for the functions they serve poses a problem that is undoubtedly complex. In some instances they involve a literal surrender, in others an escape, in others an identification, in others a desire to be accepted and to belong, in others a quest for a more meaningful life. They can vary all the way from infantile dependency upon a parental substitute to a superstitious veneration of an allegedly holy man. In general they represent what has been commonly described as hero worship, but their complexity transcends this well-known category. Always there is a continuity of self-interest between the devotee and the idolized person, with the latter in some respects the extension or enlargement of the psyche of the former. But apart from this, the role of significant persons in the lives of others, which under certain circumstances is absolutized into a form of idolatry, is far from understood and constitutes one of the deep and persistent problems of human society. It is no surprise, therefore, that a modern psychologist, observing the manner in which his clients responded to him, should comment in the significant words, "Because so many people have asked me to be their god, I have come to appreciate the significance of a real god." [1]

The transformation of a pastor into an object of idolatrous loyalty seems to follow similar lines. If he is potentially qualified as a hero, his immediacy accelerates the process. As a living image who moves about he has an advantage over the graven image of the conventional pagan. If he is categorized as a holy man, the advantage is even greater. He is there before the people. He is in their midst as a person — a visible symbol of the faith they profess. The Jesus of history is more remote. Even for the Corinthian congregation, a generation separated them from his crucifixion, and Palestine was far away — a land of different customs and of a different outlook on life. As for the modern congregation, two thousand years is a great interval of time, not to speak of the radical changes that distinguish their perspective from that of the ancient past. Consequently the Jesus of history is apt to be regarded as a strange, shadowy figure of the past whom they only vaguely know through a book. The pastor who speaks to them and interprets the book seems nearer. They see him frequently. They work with him. They become attached to him and depend upon him. They become emotionally involved with him. Thus, under these circumstances it is easy to confuse their loyalty to him with loyalty to Christ. They come to hear him rather than Christ. They join the church only for him.

In such an idolatrous relationship between pastor and people we have the modern form of the problem of the idolatrous loyalties of the opening chapters of First Corinthians. As such it is a major problem — perhaps the most difficult pastoral problem of all, the one that every pastor and congregation must solve if they are truly to worship, to live as Christians, and to proclaim the gospel. In other words, it has to do with their understanding of the contemporaneity of Christ. It concerns the peculiar temptation of the pastor, either through his connivance or theirs, to come between them and Christ. He presumes to become their Lord instead of remaining a servant of Christ.

But the error of idolatrous loyalties always has its counter-part in the error of spiritual leaders whose love of recognition encourages them. The prospect of followers who will boast of them as some boasted of Paul, Apollos, and Cephas so flatters them that they cannot refrain from building up themselves instead of the church. As a consequence of this weakness, they win followers to themselves and not to Christ, and by a curious distortion of spirit mistake such loyalty for faith in Christ. What they achieve, of course, presupposes the exploitation of an art as old as man's attempts to influence others for his own ends, which in Corinth was the legacy of a long tradition of specialization. Paul's name for it was *sophia logou,* which may be variously rendered " wisdom of words," " eloquent wisdom," " clever reasoning," or " persuasive speech." In Corinth it meant the skill of professional rhetoric associated with sophistry — a skill undoubtedly attractive to politicians and others with a vested interest in the art of persuasion. In the modern scene the probable equivalent is less likely polished oratory than the art which in colloquial phraseology is described as " putting something across," and which insofar as it wins a following is the art of " putting oneself across."

It was this art which Paul condemned as incompatible with faith in the crucified Christ. He had given it no place in his ministry, and according to his appraisal of Apollos and Cephas they had given it no place in theirs. He had rejected it because the mode of communicating the gospel cannot be inconsistent with the nature of the gospel. The means of grace cannot be incompatible with the meaning of grace. Love can be communicated only by love, forgiveness only by forgiveness, and Christ only by the Holy Spirit. The message of the cross would be nullified if communicated by all the devices of appeal and argument peculiar to the ancient sophists or the modern advertisers — those professional persuaders who pride themselves on the ability to sell almost anything. Under these circumstances the cross would be emptied of its power (I Cor. 1:17).

The precise identification of the error of the idolatrous loyalties and of this reprehensible art may be inferred from Paul's three strongly worded questions: " Is Christ divided? Was Paul crucified for you? Or were you baptized in the name of Paul? " The significant fact is that these questions focus directly upon the Christological center of the pastoral problem, namely, what happens to Christ when his people are attracted more to ministers than to him. They are questions that concern the threat to the ultimate truth content of the gospel when the people of the church profess Christian faith for no other reason than the fact that they like the minister.

According to the first question, idolatrous faith in ministers is a potentially divisive faith, whether it be an emotional attachment to a local pastor or a more extensive devotion to a great name in the history of the church. Its divisiveness concerns Christ himself. It divides him up, or parcels him out, presumably to each contending party. The seriousness derives from Paul's emphasis on the presence of Christ in the church, qualifying it as his body. Dividing up Christ or dismembering the body of Christ is tantamount to the death of the body. It is comparable to the destruction of the temple of God which Paul contemplates a little later in the letter where he identifies the temple with the Corinthians themselves as the abode of the divine presence (ch. 3:16-17). Dividing up Christ can only mean crucifying him afresh and destroying the fellowship (koinonia) that he creates, or more specifically, annihilating the love (agape) that inspires it. This is not an inappropriate description of strife in the church, in view of the lasting effects upon the participants. They drive God out of their lives, so that the ultimate consequences are often as atheistic as the crudest unbelief, regardless of the religious passion that motivates them (cf. I John 3:14-15).

The second question may be understood as a warning to the Corinthians of the manner in which they accomplish this unfortunate result. The warning is implied in the strongly negative answer that the form of the question demands. " Was Paul crucified for you? " The implication is that the Corinthians were substituting the idolized minister at the place where

even the thought of the possibility would seem enough to forbid it. This was at the cross, where the death of Christ procured the forgiveness of sins. Since it is improbable that the
error would be conscious or deliberate, it would apparently
arise out of the temptation to regard Paul as the founder of the
faith, which, like the temptation to regard any minister as normative of orthodoxy, would have this effect. It was the temptation to hear his word instead of the word of Christ through
him and to see his sacrifice instead of the sacrifice of Christ to
which it testified. The practical form of the danger may be
illustrated from Christian experience when the people put their
faith in a minister. When they discover that he is only a man
and indeed a sinner, their faith is shattered. When they build
the life and work of the church around him only to lose him
through death or other circumstances, their church collapses.
In these eventualities, his role as a lesser Christ who in effect
has been offering forgiveness in his own name exposes him as a
substitute for the crucified Christ at the point of ultimate concern.

But there was another way in which the Corinthians were
dividing up Christ and destroying him. This appears in their
conception of the minister as a supplement to Christ, as implied in the third question: " Were you baptized in the name of
Paul? " It involved the minister's coming between the believer
and Christ as an idol whose special power is presumed to contribute to the creation of faith. It means procuring for himself
surreptitiously through baptism the role of an intermediary, as
if by the sacred rite he could add his power to that of the Holy
Spirit.

Paul's expanded comment on baptism indicates the seriousness of such a problem in Corinth. Some seem to have prided
themselves on baptism at the hands of their favorite apostle, as
if to suggest that their loyalty to him was in some respect derivative of it. Although nothing more is said of the falsity of
their conception, a plausible explanation appears in the practice
of some of the mystery cults, in which it was believed that a
mystical rapport was established between the baptizer and the

baptized by virtue of his administration of the rite.[2] This would explain Paul's emphasis on the fact that he had baptized none of the Corinthians except Crispus and Gaius and the household of Stephanas. It would also explain his claim that Christ commissioned him not to baptize but to preach the gospel. He is not here denying the validity or the importance of baptism but only the inclination to give it priority over the communication of the gospel. More particularly he is denying such an interpretation of it as would transform the minister into a supplement to Christ.

III

THE FOLLY OF WORLDLY WISDOM

1 *For the word of the cross is folly to those who are perishing, but to us who are being saved it is the power of God.* ¹⁹ *For it is written,*

> *" I will destroy the wisdom of the wise,*
> *and the cleverness of the clever I will thwart."*

²⁰ *Where is the wise man? Where is the scribe? Where is the debater of this age? Has not God made foolish the wisdom of the world?* ²¹ *For since, in the wisdom of God, the world did not know God through wisdom, it pleased God through the folly of what we preach to save those who believe.*

The abrupt introduction of worldly wisdom at this point may create the impression that Paul has left the problem of the idolatrous loyalties behind. There is no stated connection between the one theme and the other that would explain the transition. At one moment he is deploring the fact that some say, " I belong to Paul," " I belong to Apollos "; at another moment he is declaring that God will destroy the wisdom of the wise. Consequently, it may be overlooked that the idolatrous loyalties remain as the primary theme of the first four chapters and condition all the secondary themes that Paul finds it necessary to weave into his material. The manner in which he keeps returning to these loyalties throughout his presentation, and his repeated warnings against the boasting of men which they represent, are sufficient confirmation of this fact (chs. 1:31; 3:3-4, 21-23; 4:6-7).

The worldly wisdom against which Paul contends is clearly antithetical to the gospel. Its devotees regard the word of the cross as foolishness. The implication is that this prompts them to reject the crucified Christ in favor of idolatrous loyalties to the various ministers of Christ who had labored among them. In this respect the worldly wisdom is contributory to these loyalties and may be considered their spiritual source. To deal with them in an adequate manner, it is necessary for Paul to direct his attention to the worldly wisdom responsible for them. As a false form of faith, worldly wisdom was the real competitor of the gospel in the Corinthian church.

But what was this wisdom? What were its characteristics? Since the term had a wide variety of meaning, and a history which in Hebraic and Hellenic civilization was indicative of the ethos of particular periods, pursuits, and perspectives of life, to conceive of it in a general manner is not sufficient. Paul's polemic against it is too specific and practical to regard it as only a climate of opinion or as an atmosphere of thought. Moreover, it is unlikely that the peculiar form in which it confronted him in Corinth could be described as a philosophy of religion or as a philosophy in the technical sense. The proletarian character of the people constituting the church, not many of whom were wise according to worldly standards, and not many of whom were powerful or of noble birth, would not favor the view that the wisdom popular among them was of a highly intellectual character. Possessed of appeal at the common level and communicable by the persuasive art of sophistry (chs. 1:17, 20; 2:1, 4, 13), it was probably a mixture akin to theosophy (cf. Col. 2:8, 16-23) and qualified to a greater or lesser extent by gnosticism (I Cor. 8:1-3, 11; 12:3; 13:2). The Corinthians would be familiar with it in one form or another either from professional sophists or from the many itinerant teachers of the time, many of whom were interested more in applause, riches, and fame than in the truth.

In such wisdom Paul detected a deep and persistent pride that was characterized by an idolatrous confidence in men and

that for this reason encouraged a similar confidence in the
various ministers who had labored in the Corinthian congregation. He describes it as a pride that boasted of men in the presence of God (ch. 1:29) instead of boasting in the Lord (ch.
1:31; cf. Gal. 6:14). It exulted in the boldness of the sophists,
who could improvise on a subject at a moment's notice and
whose eloquence impressed the gullible mind not only as clever
but as inspired (I Cor. 2:4-5). It was a pride that was crafty
and vain in its thoughts, so that if the Corinthians were to build
their faith on the crucified Christ as the only foundation (ch.
3:11), they had no other alternative but to renounce all such
boasting in men (ch. 3:21). It was provocative of jealousy and
strife (ch. 3:3), and of a puffed-up attitude toward one minister of Christ over against another (ch. 4:6). Briefly, it was a
pride that was the antithesis of genuine love (ch. 13:4-5; cf.
ch. 8:1-3).

The situation which therefore confronted Paul was one in
which the Corinthians regarded " the Christian message as wisdom like that of the Greeks, the Christian leaders as teachers of
wisdom, themselves as wise, and all this to boast about." [3] In
this respect their conception of the servant of God was only
an extension of their own egotism and a protection against the
evangelical offense of the cross. What they saw in him was
determined only by their religious likes and dislikes and not by
the truth, which would have compelled a painful reappraisal
of these. It was similar to the popularization of a minister
whose message appeals to his people because they hear only
what they wish to hear and in this manner have their religious
opinions and prejudices confirmed. It probably bore a resemblance to those indefinable qualities of personal attraction
which may vary all the way from an infatuation and a mere
transference of emotion to a mystical appeal, each as undisciplined by the gospel as the others.

The problem thus constituted by worldly wisdom within
the Corinthian church was, however, only a special instance of
the same problem within the world. The idolatrous exaltation
of religious leaders was only a special instance of the idolatrous

exaltation of men. It was consistent with the dictum of the sophists that man is the measure of all things, and with the dogma of modern atheists that man's only hope is in himself. In the connotation of religion, it ultimately reduces itself to the equation of faith in man with faith in God, which, as it pertains to the vanity of the individual, is the equation of self-confidence with faith in God.

In certain periods of history this idolatrous inclination is stronger. These are the periods in which the individual experiences the loss of economic security and personal significance. For him, great ideas are of less appeal than great persons, because of the promise of help the latter provide. Under these circumstances, mass movements are organized around great personalities, especially those who qualify as strong men. The significant fact seems to be that their great achievements answer to the loss of face sustained by adverse circumstances, as much as they answer to economic need.

But the extent to which idolatrous relationships with signficant persons characterize the life of the average man even in less critical times at once indicates the fertile soil in which the more extreme forms take root and flourish. Consistent with this fact is that the more the possession of an acceptable personality becomes a factor in secular success, the greater the likelihood that at some future date the whole society will be organized around one leading personality in an idolatrous subservience to him. And the same could be said of the church. Indeed, to know or praise the right man at the right time — the wise, the mighty, the well-born according to the system or civilization to which they belong — seems always to have been an important qualification of worldly wisdom. At the ordinary level it is consistent with the emphasis, in the best worldly wisdom, on skill, art, intuition, and on how to achieve, control, or influence beyond the limits of science or knowledge as such.

But even within these limits it concerns the idolatrous confidence in the expert, who becomes an object of ultimate trust apart from the possession of personality. The mathematician, the scientist, the surgeon, the genius and the maestro, the brain trust, or the automated image of man are so many equivalents of the philosopher-king. As gods many and lords many, they add their testimony to the fact that worldly wisdom is more than a conniving form of prudence at the personal level. It enters into the best that men can achieve and conditions the impression left upon their followers.

When, therefore, Paul warned, " Let no man boast of men " (I Cor. 3:21), his words pertained to a wider constituency than the Corinthian congregation or the church universal, just as the same could be said of the words of his Old Testament predecessor: " Cursed is the man who trusts in man and makes flesh his arm, whose heart turns away from the Lord " (Jer. 17:5). The words pertained to all forms of confidence that absolutize man individually or collectively, in which the resultant claim upon the follower is total in its scope. They had no reference to the normal confidence in others vital to social relationships and without which society in any form would be impossible. They concerned only that absolutizing of man which was disruptive of social relationships, as the dissensions in the Corinthian church suggested.

It was disruptive of these relationships because of its self-contradictory character, which, as already indicated, was antithetical to the gospel. This was the strange paradox of a pride by which men are prompted to resist the best and accept the worst even to the point of perishing, and to justify their action as good and reasonable. It was essentially the mystery of man against himself, which neither morality nor science has been able to resolve. The clinician sees it in the self-contradictory life of his patient, parents in the blind love of a marriagable son or daughter, statesmen in the selfish interests of an electorate, and historians in the inability of a ruling class to see the injustices of their policy.

The story of this subtle, complex pride and of the history and culture associated with it involves the concealment of evil under a form of goodness. This emerges as a rationalization of the fundamental idolatry, which is always motivated by the greatest variety of self-justification. Thus the most dangerous forms of evil are not those visible and plain to see, about which all are agreed and against which laws are enacted, but those concealed beneath a worldly complex of righteousness and rationality. This is why open theft, although dangerous, is not as great a menace to society as stealing with the law; open falsehood not as great a threat to public integrity as lying within the truth; open hatred not as great a disturbance to human relationships as hatred within the holy. In each instance an implicit self-justification is productive of an elaborate structure of rationalization. Everyone has his reasons in defense of a spurious righteousness. The corrupt politician insists upon the justice of his actions, the unscrupulous advertiser upon the excellence of his products, and the facile journalist upon the high quality of his editorials. All the profiteers have their reasons for high prices, just as the promoters of religion or irreligion have their reasons for the particular cause they serve. Considering, therefore, the whole complex of this rationalization, it is evident that here is a form of sophistry, with its art of persuasion, designed for no other purpose than the perpetuation of itself. If in the modern world this be called the philosophy of success, it is only another name for the wisdom of the world. As such, it not only involves pride as a moral or psychological category but as a symptom of unbelief.

Paul was convinced that God would destroy the wisdom that inspired an idolatrous loyalty to men. He was certain of this because the word of the cross as the power of God had destroyed the worldly wisdom in his own life. He could point, moreover, to the history of his people, where he found testimony to the same power of God in the same destructive capacity. " For it is written, ' I will destroy the wisdom of the wise, and the cleverness of the clever I will thwart.' " The allusion is to an event in the history of Israel in which the prophet Isaiah was confronted with a problem similar to the one that confronted Paul in Corinth. The event was the siege of Jerusalem by the Assyrians under Sennacherib. Popular confidence in the wisdom of political leaders and counselors had reached the point where it discouraged faith in the possibility of divine deliverance as advocated by the prophet. Even though it led to despair, the confidence remained unbroken. But in the midst of popular gloom, in a strange turn of events, the siege was suddenly lifted and the city saved, contrary to the worldly wisdom of the leaders and counselors. This amounted to a remarkable confirmation of the faith of the prophet and was never forgotten in the annals of Jewish history.

In this incident, which Paul regarded as prophetic of the situation in Corinth, as both were prophetic of human history as a whole, was the same idolatrous confidence in men, the same worldly wisdom as its foundation, and the same urgency. The urgency in Corinth derived from Paul's eschatological perspective in which the present age is at its end, as Jerusalem was at the time of the siege except for the intervention of God.

The manner in which this ancient deliverance illustrates how God makes foolish the wisdom of the world explains the triumphant tone of the questions that follow: " Where is the wise man? Where is the scribe? Where is the debater of this age? " Such men as these would probably be idolized because of the popular recognition of their authority, but the significant fact is the extent to which the action of God in the events of history, belies their predictions. Things have a way of turning out so differently from what the authorities of the age have predicted that if public memory were not so short, a serious deterioration of confidence would result. There is an irony of history which shatters the secure world of accepted ideas and the comfortable expectations of men no matter how plausible these may sound upon the lips of experts. In terms of modern experience it may be recalled that the great statesmen, historians, and philosophers who stood on the threshold of the twentieth century scarcely saw the shape of things to come. Few discerned the signs of the times even at the dawn of the first great unprecedented war. In a strange manner the wisest men of the world, apart from natural limitations of knowledge, are made to look foolish by the unfolding drama of history. It reveals the extent to which their wisdom is only a rationalizing of the self-interest of the society to which they belong and therefore is too arrogant in its logic to appreciate the tragic paradoxes of life.[4] It reveals this in a manner which leaves them no alternative but to reap what they have sown, even though they do not recognize what they have sown. In this respect God makes foolish the wisdom of the world by so ordering existence as to compel the fruition of its pride (cf. Rom. 7:13). This does not mean that the events of history are equivalent to the will of God or that the contingencies of life are the same as his action. But these may possess a significance that reveals them as more than events and contingencies, indeed as signs of the movement of God by which in a mysterious way his wonders are performed, as the lifting of the siege of Jerusalem testified.

But there is a further aspect of the way in which worldly wisdom is revealed as foolishness. This is suggested by the similarity between Paul's conception of such wisdom and that of Ecclesiastes, in which its pride results in emptiness (Eccl. 2:1-17). When worldly wisdom is conceived as an ultimate objective in life, it fails in the end to satisfy the deepest longing of the human heart. The wise man dies as the fool, his wisdom helpless to provide the answer to the enigma of death. Indeed, the wisdom that seeks perfection without purpose and efficiency without faith, and is thereby devoted more and more to itself as the chief objective in life, is exposed not only as emptiness (boredom) but as a form of death (*taedium vitae*). In this way the pride of wisdom in its self-seeking, whether it be of the individual or of the collective, tends to be self-defeating. The reaction to its meaninglessness is either that of a radical hatred (Eccl. 2:17) or the emergence of a faith which realizes that the world by wisdom does not know God (I Cor. 1:21; cf. Eccl. 1:18; 3:11b).

The insight of Ecclesiastes at this point is consistent with Paul's understanding that God makes foolish the wisdom of the world. Such wisdom, by its promotion of an idolatrous confidence in men, only succeeds in the production of hollow men.[5] What happens to wisdom along with pleasure, wine, achievement, and possessions as the chief objectives in life happens to men as objects of idolatrous devotion. They themselves become as empty in relation to what their devotees expect of them as these goals themselves.

But at this point it is important to sound a warning. God in his wisdom does not oblige a man to see through the wisdom of the world in order to be confronted by nothingness — on the strange supposition that this would be faith. Nor does he oblige a man to see through himself and his fellowmen, as if by such insight the resulting disillusionment would be equivalent to faith. Faith is not such in its nature that it requires a man to live on the basis of negativism. There is no inherent significance in a man's coming to the end of his resources or hitting the bottom (relatively speaking) of the mysterious depths of life. Modern nihilism, which encourages the latter as a secular equivalent of faith, is only another form of worldly wisdom. It embodies the pride of man in negative form — as if out of a hatred of life this were its peculiar mission (Eccl. 2:17). It is important to sound such a warning because it is clear from Paul's statement of the divine purpose in the negation of worldly wisdom that it was not to disillusion man as a nihilistic objective but to point him to the gospel. The purpose was positive, with the negative only of such a nature as to be of service to the positive. This may be seen from the latter part of I Cor. 1:21, which reads in its entirety, " For since, in the wisdom of God, the world did not know God through [its] wisdom, it pleased God through the folly of what we preach to save those who believe."

IV

THE OFFENSE OF THE CROSS
1:22 to 2:5

1 *For Jews demand signs and Greeks seek wisdom,* [23] *but we preach Christ crucified, a stumbling block to Jews and folly to Gentiles,* [24] *but to those who are called, both Jews and Greeks, Christ the power of God and the wisdom of God.* [25] *For the foolishness of God is wiser than men, and the weakness of God is stronger than men.*

26 *For consider your call, brethren; not many of you were wise according to worldly standards, not many were powerful, not many were of noble birth;* [27] *but God chose what is foolish in the world to shame the wise, God chose what is weak in the world to shame the strong,* [28] *God chose what is low and despised in the world, even things that are not, to bring to nothing things that are,* [29] *so that no human being might boast in the presence of God.* [30] *He is the source of your life in Christ Jesus, whom God made our wisdom, our righteousness and sanctification and redemption;* [31] *therefore, as it is written, "Let him who boasts, boast of the Lord."*

2 *When I came to you, brethren, I did not come proclaiming to you the testimony of God in lofty words or wisdom.* [2] *For I decided to know nothing among you except Jesus Christ and him crucified.* [3] *And I was with you in weakness and in much fear and trembling;* [4] *and my speech and my message were not in plausible words of wisdom, but in demonstration of the Spirit and power,* [5] *that your faith might not rest in the wisdom of men but in the power of God.*

Paul now turns his attention to the standards by which worldly wisdom determines the object of its idolatrous loyalty. He is concerned with how it selects the particular apostle, minister, or religiously significant person, or for that matter the hero or type most worthy of its confidence. This is his purpose in speaking of the Jewish demand for signs and the Greek quest for wisdom. In the context of his problem such a demand or quest defines the quality of the person who merits their respective loyalties. The Jews demand a sign as proof of inspiration — a demonstration by the prophet, teacher, or religious leader that he possesses miraculous power and that God authenticates him by means of it. Illustrations of the demand appear in the Gospels, where Jesus is frequently asked for a sign by his interrogators. The Greek quest for wisdom fulfills a similar purpose. This is a means of evaluating the spirituality of any man whose appearance attracts attention as possibly possessed of religious significance and who for this reason might be worthy of devotion. This spirituality pertains to a quality characteristic of the developed mind and spirit of man and is indicative of the highest expression of what is human.

The modern man no less than the ancient Jew or Greek has his standards of religious loyalty. Popular expectations of what constitutes a religiously significant person in a community or of the proper role of a minister will suggest several familiar illustrations. Among the religious sects, for example, the requirement may be similar to the ancient demand for a demonstration of miraculous (charismatic) power. Among more highly institutionalized religious bodies, the same demand may be met not by a demonstration but by simply regarding the spiritual leader as already possessed of power and therefore worthy of loyalty by virtue of his office. Or the standard of loyalty may be closer to that of the ancient Greeks. In this instance, apart from the balance and common sense expected of the spiritual leader, it may pertain to his education or practical judgment as an administrator or counselor. Or the standard of loyalty may bear a resemblance to that of the Jew and the Greek in the manner in which it combines a peculiar power with a peculiar wisdom, as seen in the extent to which the possession of a popular personality has become the measure of spirituality.

The standards of the Jews and Greeks, however, were the basis of judgment by which Christ was rejected as one worthy of religious devotion. Popular Jewish expectations of a political Messiah, for example, often dictated that he exhibit the grandiose signs of an apocalyptic deliverer who would destroy the enemies of Israel and establish her as an eternal kingdom on earth. As a strong man fulfilling the alleged purposes of God by such evidence of victory as that suggested by the threefold temptation — turning stones into bread, working unheard-of wonders, and conquering the kingdoms of the earth (Matt. 4:1-11) — he would be a miracle man whom popular loyalty would espouse with an idolatrous zeal. A Christ who would not yield to such a purpose and become an instrument of national pride would be rejected, more especially as he called for repentance and made unqualified demands of discipleship.

In his quest for wisdom, the Greek was no less offended by such a Christ than the Jew. To have this highest quality of human development exposed as incapable of freeing man from the possibility of sin seemed a ridiculous judgment. To be confronted by one who called the wise to himself not as one who acknowledged the possession of wisdom in common with them but as one who identified himself with its ultimate form seemed only the action of a fool. For the common variety of sophist, who could prove anything for a price, it exposed the fact that rationality was as effective as religion in the concealment of selfish interests. This is indicative of why all forms of wisdom — higher and lower — were offended at Christ.

Along with these ancient standards of the Jews and Greeks, modern standards of religious loyalty are also capable of rejecting and crucifying Christ. The same pride of power and the same concealment of selfish interest by means of a higher quality of human development (culture) generally obtain. In this matter the expectations of a congregation, which determine the acceptability of a minister, are no exception. The frequent preference for a quality of life that is pleasantly acceptable to all but is actually without significance can only mean that a congregation convinced of this standard would be deeply offended at the call to take up the cross and follow Christ in its original, authentic meaning.

What the modern man has in common with the ancient Jew and Greek is an unshakable confidence in his standards of religious loyalty, which for obvious reasons are inevitably his standards of divinity. He is confident he knows what God is like, or should be like. But in this confidence, as Paul had discovered in his personal experience (Phil. 3:4-6) and in that of the Corinthian congregation, was a deeply rooted pride which, though capable of serious religious expression, was actually the dynamic of worldly wisdom and therefore fundamentally in opposition to God. Such pride so qualified the standards of loyalty that in practice it virtually defined them no matter how Biblical, theological, or philosophical their theoretical formulation might be.

Consequently, when men saw what God was like he was so different from their conceptions of him that most of them thought of him not as God but as a criminal whom they condemned to death and executed. Convinced that they believed in God, as a modern poll of public opinion might have confirmed, they were so outraged by the reality of God in their midst that they could not endure him. Some could only regard him as utterly evil and radically antithetical to all that was holy (Mark 3:22). Thus the paradoxical character of such a strange event is evident the more seriously we recognize that its instigators were religious men who in the name of God had acted to preserve his sanctity. Confident of themselves as chosen of him and equally confident of their knowledge of Scripture and sacred tradition, upon which they thought they had based their judgment, they could not tolerate his real presence among them. Even those whose ordained status indicated their conception of themselves as ministers of God took the initiative in putting him to death. In this respect the crucified Christ may be regarded as the criminal Christ and his cross representative of God among men under the sign of criminality.

The surprise which comes of the thought that such men would destroy God, when we have always believed that only the irreligious would destroy him, strains our normal comprehension. It contradicts the popular conviction that faith in God of any variety, however vague, nebulous, or confessionally insignificant, would never dream of such dreadful action. It also contradicts the conviction current in the ancient and modern world that man in the higher ranges of his mind and spirit is nearer to God than he is in those lower ranges of passion and desire where irrationality predominates. The thought of the primal sin of man finding its locus in the spirit of man in prompting a destructive attitude toward God and therefore as the ultimate source of human destructiveness will be difficult to entertain. Yet how does one reconcile the mystery of man's inhumanity to man with those higher values which in practical life are regarded by all peoples as their ultimate loyalty? Or if this seems too theoretical, it may be sufficient only to consider the extent to which a person possessed of faith and of a knowledge of Scripture and tradition will be violently opposed to the thought of what is ultimately the best for him and shout it down as if it were foreign to him. All churches are familiar enough with this phenomenon within their midst to understand why godly men in the name of God should seek to destroy God.

The quality of the offense experienced by the Jew was different, however, from that experienced by the Greek. For one, the crucified Christ was a stumbling block (scandal), for the other, foolishness. This meant for the one that the crucified Christ was an insult and therefore to be denied; for the other, he was irrelevant and therefore to be ignored. The difference that qualified their experience can be interpreted only in the light of their respective standards of judgment. As we have already seen, the fact that the Jew found in the crucified Christ a stumbling block presupposes the Jewish theology of signs. In keeping with the tenets of Hebraism, which emphasized the difference between God and man, these signs or miracles were regarded as criteria of difference. For this reason the Jews were prepared for a Messiah who was different, but not for one as different as this. They were not prepared for one so different that he was God incarnate — really God, in whom Messiahship and deity coalesced. According to their conception of monotheism, the chief source of offense was the ascription of deity to Christ (cf. John 5:18; 10:33). It denied what they considered to be the sovereignty and transcendence of God and opened the door to what they regarded as a new form of paganism centered in the worship of a man (cf. idolatrous loyalty). But the awful thought of ascribing deity to a man executed as a criminal, and to think of the crime as committed by the chosen people of God, was worse than blasphemous. It was the worst possible insult.

In Greek philosophy, with its variety of problems and points of view, the tendency was in the opposite direction. An emphasis on unity instead of difference, the unity of man with God (gods) and nature, at least as a theoretical possibility, defined their quest for truth. Accordingly, the master conception definitive of wisdom was always a form of harmony — equilibrium, paradox, temperance, tolerance, compromise, compensation — and at the ordinary level common sense and reasonableness. Consequently, the Greeks did not think of a divine man (incarnation) as embodying a differential but a quality or power which in principle was similar to that in every man. What offended them, therefore, was the exclusive claim that Jesus was the Christ, beside whom there was no other. For this was a claim which carried with it the implicit intolerance of other lords and religions, and which at the fundamental point was incompatible with the traditional Greek concern for unity. As one who on this account was crucified, it violated the rational and was therefore regarded as a radical form of foolishness.

It is important, however, to remember that the source of offense to Jews and Greeks was not only the crucified Christ but the gospel that Paul preached concerning him. The offense of the cross which they experienced was a reaction to both. The essential consideration was that Paul proclaimed the death of Christ as the deliverance of men from the bondage of guilt. This meant that his death was the one, all-sufficient sacrifice for sin. A few representative texts will confirm this fact, namely: " Christ died for our sins in accordance with the scriptures " (I Cor. 15:3); " He made him to be sin who knew no sin, so that in him we might become the righteousness of God " (II Cor. 5:21); " Christ redeemed us from the curse of the law, having become a curse for us " (Gal. 3:13); " God shows his love for us in that while we were yet sinners Christ died for us " (Rom. 5:8). Those Jews and Greeks who were offended could not acknowledge that they were guilty before God to the extent that the death of such a man in such a manner should be the only means of eternal forgiveness for them. They could not acknowledge their inextricable involvement in guilt as the fundamental problem of their existence.

The Jew, however, could acknowledge his guilt on the basis of the difference that he recognized between man and God, this time as a difference for which man was responsible, namely, his sin. But he thought it was manageable either through the cultus as it provided sacrifice for sin or through repentance, which was regarded as a meritorious act acceptable to God. To put forth the crucified Christ as the exclusive means of resolving his guilt was therefore an insult to his cultus and to his capacity for repentance.

In contrast to the Jews, the Greeks gave less if any essential place to guilt as a fundamental problem of existence. This was undoubtedly related to their emphasis on the unity between God (gods) and man, which permitted no serious consideration of the disruption of the unity from the side of man. Consequently, the Greek could not acknowledge guilt; still less could he acknowledge the need of the crucified Christ as the sole means of resolving it. The whole idea, as so often to the modern man, seemed irrelevant. He was more inclined, like modern man, to shift the responsibility to nature, or to his social environment, or to the God or gods behind the scenes, and therefore to speak of fate instead of guilt. In this context the Greeks could say much concerning the tragic aspect of life and the heroic quality of human existence as men unsuccessfully defied the hand of fate. And they could say much concerning the various forms of resignation to fate, concerning adjustment to life, which, according to their concept of harmony, was the best answer to the human predicament. But they could not seriously acknowledge themselves as sinners as in the Hebrew tradition at its best.

But there were other Jews and Greeks for whom the crucified Christ was the wisdom of God and the power of God (I Cor. 1:24), which is indicative of the manner in which the gospel cuts across religious, racial, and national lines. For these persons, the gospel of the crucified Christ was heard as the call of God. Indeed, Paul describes them as the called and therefore, presumably, as those who in the mysterious working of God were disposed to hear the word of the cross out of the cross. They heard it as the word of a unique love which they had never before heard, even though they had experienced love in the ordinary relationships of daily life. As a love which had identified itself with the darkest side of their life, never failing to seek them in spite of their opposition, it had dispelled their initial impression of its criminality. As those who were vulnerable to its gentle indirectness and so to the one who in loving gave himself, they had found that in his acceptance of them had come the forgiveness of God. His death as the act of such acceptance was no longer recognized as the death of a criminal but as the death of one who though innocent had assumed their guilt and taken their place. The good news of his achievement was not the proclamation of a myth that only symbolized the integration of the psychical and the elimination of the feeling of guilt. It was the proclamation of an historical event representative of the transcendental action of God and characterized by the resolution of real, objective guilt. As a miracle comparable to the creation or to the resurrection, it was spoken of by Paul as the power of God. This was the power to resolve guilt — that guilt which no man is able to remove from the life of another or to tear out of his own heart. As such, it was the resolution of that problem which is constituted by the fact that sin recedes into the past, and like the past is incapable of recall for the sake of rectification, but is always conditioning the present as the inescapable bondage of man, for which he is responsible. Those who knew

that the crucified Christ was the power of God had been released from bondage. They had received a new freedom in
Christ. At the same time they knew that the crucified Christ
was the wisdom of God because his death, by its removal of
guilt, procured their reconciliation with him, which was a
unique form of harmony. The establishment of this unity
which no man is ever able to establish by negotiation, compromise, toleration, or other form of harmony enabled them to
find a new and amazing unity with themselves and their fellowmen. Expressed in simple language, it enabled them for the
first time really to love.

If all this seemed theoretical to the Corinthians, if they
could not believe that this was really happening to them and
that the love of God for man as it actually encountered them
was the profoundest wisdom, though seemingly foolish, they
were to look at the church. Its humble constituency was the
proof of the humility of its Lord. The fact that there were
not many wise according to worldly standards, not many
powerful, not many of noble birth, was not accidental. It was
consistent with all that Paul had said of Christ and the gospel,
and a visible rebuke to those inclined to idolatrous loyalties. It
was a sign of the participation of the church in the offense of
the cross. Its derivative source and explanation was this call
which they had received. On this point Paul is most explicit:
" God chose what is foolish in the world to shame the
wise, . . . what is weak . . . to shame the strong, . . .
what is low and despised . . . , even things that are not, to
bring to nothing things that are, so that no human being might
boast in the presence of God."

If these facts were a source of embarrassment to those
whose glorying in men probably meant that they coveted a
greater number of people in the church who were important
by worldly standards, Paul left no doubt in their minds of the
normative character of their low position. It was not something of which to be ashamed or critical, as if the church
should gradually eliminate the nondescripts from its membership and replace them with the better people of the community. It was indicative of something profound, no less than

the character of the God who had called them. It was therefore indigenous to the nature of the church, and a norm of its
visibility. In this respect it was consistent with the example of
the apostles, the visibility of whose ministry included the fact
that they were weak, held in disrepute, subject to hunger and
thirst, ill clad, buffeted and homeless, and stigmatized as the
refuse of the world and the offscouring of all things.

Such visibility, in which the church participates in the offense of the cross, is often misunderstood, however, as socially
pathological, indicative only of what the enemies of Christ
describe as an exploitation of the decadence of Greco-Roman
city life. Illustrative of this more extreme reaction are the bit-
ter utterances of Nietzsche, who condemned the Christian
faith as a manifestation of the vengeance of slaves upon their
masters, a prizing of everything that society despises, a saying
of no to all that is natural, a favoring of the suffering, botched,
and degenerate, and a despising of the rich, scholarly, noble,
healthy, and strong.[6] On a wider scale the accusations of confirmed secularists are similar — that the Christian faith thwarts
the potentialities of self-realization necessary for individual
and national survival. No different in principle are the milder
reactions of the modern elite who frown upon the humility
of the Christian as a lack of refinement, or as an undignified
propensity for making all things too common.

Undoubtedly the gospel of the cross did attract the low and
despised. But this did not mean that when they realized what
it involved it was less offensive to them than to their social
superiors. Indeed, the variety of pastoral problems that confronted Paul in the Corinthian church strongly suggests that
they did not take easily to the Christian faith. Attracted at first
on the basis of its personal appeal, which was probably misconstrued by circumstance and selfish interest, the low and
despised were as resistant to the word of the cross as anyone
else when it came to ethical action and spiritual insight.

The real significance of the divine choice comes from the
peculiar love that inspires it, which is not a question of social
preference, as if for the low and despised it were meritorious

to be inferior. It is a love that demands justice — and more than justice, in all that mercy means. It is a love that negates the pride of life. The idolatrous preoccupation with self-esteem and status, and the vain deference to persons, no matter how concealed by religious fervor, must be overcome if such love is to be born within the human heart.

In the final analysis, the Christian answer to the modern critics who condemn the humility of Christianity as socially pathological is never only an argument exposing their fallacy but the fruits of the Spirit in the Christian life. Such love is its own best defense. The reality of an open, honest, reconciled relationship among men, which means their release from hatred and guilt, in which there is no longer fear of spies, secret police, and concentration camps or of hidden persuasion and brainwashing but genuine freedom, is the most powerful argument for it.

Corresponding to the offense of the cross and the offense of the church is the further fact that Paul emphasizes — the offense of his ministry. He had come among the Corinthians as one who decided to know nothing among them but Jesus Christ and him crucified. He had repudiated all forms of persuasion that would have made his message and manner of life a commendation of himself. He had not come with a display of eloquence or of worldly wisdom which presumably would have given him status before the wise of the world, before the powerful and noble of birth, such as a sophist might have achieved or a preacher concerned only to be a " success " and not a servant of Christ. He was with the Corinthians in weakness and in much fear and trembling (ch. 2:3). The weakness probably derived from the knowledge that he was one of those whom God had chosen to shame the strong, a man formerly of influence but now despised and rejected (cf. Phil. 3:1-6). The fear and trembling probably came of the knowledge that God was present and working through him just as he had called him. In this as later in the letter the same awareness of mission undoubtedly possessed him (I Cor. 9:16; cf. Jer. 20:9).

V

THE NORMATIVE WISDOM OF GOD

2 *Yet among the mature we do impart wisdom, although it is not a wisdom of this age or of the rulers of this age, who are doomed to pass away.* [7] *But we impart a secret and hidden wisdom of God, which God decreed before the ages for our glorification.* [8] *None of the rulers of this age understood this; for if they had, they would not have crucified the Lord of glory.* [9] *But, as it is written,*

> *" What no eye has seen, nor ear heard,*
> *nor the heart of man conceived,*
> *what God has prepared for those who love him,"*

[10] *God has revealed to us through the Spirit. For the Spirit searches everything, even the depths of God.* [11] *For what person knows a man's thoughts except the spirit of the man which is in him? So also no one comprehends the thoughts of God except the Spirit of God.* [12] *Now we have received not the spirit of the world, but the Spirit which is from God, that we might understand the gifts bestowed on us by God.* [13] *And we impart this in words not taught by human wisdom but taught by the Spirit, interpreting spiritual truths to those who possess the Spirit.*

[14] *The unspiritual man does not receive the gifts of the Spirit of God, for they are folly to him, and he is not able to understand them because they are spiritually discerned.* [15] *The spiritual man judges all things, but is himself to be judged by no one.* [16] *" For who has known the mind of the Lord so as to instruct him? " But we have the mind of Christ.*

3 *But I, brethren, could not address you as spiritual men, but as men of the flesh, as babes in Christ.* [2] *I fed you with milk, not solid*

*food; for you were not ready for it; and even yet you are not
ready,* [8] *for you are still of the flesh. For while there is jealousy
and strife among you, are you not of the flesh, and behaving like
ordinary men?* [4] *For when one says, "I belong to Paul," and
another, "I belong to Apollos," are you not merely men?*

At this point in the letter Paul turns his attention away from
worldly wisdom as the productive source of idolatrous loyalties
to that true wisdom which is the wisdom of God. Although
he has previously identified it with the action of God in history
(ch. 1:20-21) and with the crucified Christ (ch. 1:24), he
now identifies it with the work of the Holy Spirit (ch. 2:10)
in what is unmistakably a Trinitarian conception. His purpose,
if one may judge from the trend of his thought, is to provide
a positive answer to the problem of idolatrous loyalties. Hitherto he has been mainly concerned with the negation of the
worldly wisdom out of which they arose. Now he is concerned
with the affirmation of the divine wisdom normative of all
loyalties. His identification of it with the work of the Holy
Spirit, which in the second chapter fills out the Trinitarian
conception, is of importance because it has a particular bearing
upon this purpose. It concerns the role of the Holy Spirit in the
communication of the wisdom of God and at once indicates
that the problem of idolatrous loyalties is essentially a problem of communication. An idolatrous loyalty occurs when
there is no genuine breaking through from God to man, when
man is in bondage to a vanity that requires such loyalty for its
security and satisfaction. This means, of course, that the transformation of an idolatrous loyalty into one that is true is not
essentially a psychological phenomenon, wholly explained by
human possibilities, but a response to the wisdom of God
which his Spirit communicates from beyond. At this point the
fundamental problem of the idolatrous loyalties and of the
worldly wisdom out of which they arise has clearly emerged.
It concerns the ultimate norm of faith in Christ — whether
such faith has validity through genuine revelation or whether

its validity is relative only to the persuasive power of Paul, Apollos, Cephas, or other spiritually significant persons. In practice the problem concerns the question of whether the people are hearing God or only the preacher. On the extent to which this represents the theme not only of the second chapter but of the first four chapters of the letter, Barth makes this significant comment: " What Christianity is especially concerned about is Christian knowledge; not about this and that, about things, even though they be last things, but about the Either-Or, the understanding or the failure to understand the three words *apo tou theou* [from God]. Unless everything deceives, this is the trend of Paul's utterance." [7]

The emphasis on communication, which for this reason is conspicuous in the section extending from chs. 2:6 to 3:4, will be recognized from the references to the impartation of divine wisdom (ch. 2:6, 7, 10, 12, 13). In such action a distinction emerges between two kinds of believers, the babes in Christ and the mature, who differ in their receptivity of the wisdom of God. The former, whose indulgence in idolatrous loyalties characterizes them as a group, are resistant to the wisdom of God and are unable to receive it. The latter, who are not disposed to such loyalties, are open to his wisdom and receive it (chs. 2:6; 3:1). The difference between them ultimately concerns their receptivity of the Holy Spirit.

What Paul means by the wisdom of God imparted among the mature (ch. 2:6) is less likely doctrine or didactic interpretation subsequent to the hearing of the gospel than the effectual hearing of the gospel. Several considerations favor this conclusion. (1) The identification of such wisdom in ch. 2:7 as secret and hidden, which " God decreed before the ages for our glorification," would indicate, according to other references, its equivalence to the gospel of grace. In Col. 1:26, for example, the Word of God which is the gospel is called " the mystery hidden for ages and generations but now made manifest to his saints." A similar equation of the mystery of the will of God with the gospel of grace appears in Ephesians, where it is said that " we have redemption . . . according to the riches of his grace. . . . For he has made known to us in all wisdom and insight the mystery of his will " (Eph. 1:7-10; cf. 2:11-16). As such the wisdom of God is without partiality to the merits of men, as worldly standards of loyalty conceive them. (2) The failure of the " rulers of this age " — possibly a reference to the demonic powers associated with world authorities — to understand this wisdom, which as a consequence caused them to crucify Christ (I Cor. 2:8), would indicate that they had not understood the Christ event as the event of grace. Their failure could hardly have been a failure to understand doctrine or didactic interpretation subsequent to the hearing of the gospel, inasmuch as their failure related to the hearing the gospel. They had not understood that the crucified Christ was the wisdom of God. (3) The identification of the crucified Christ with the wisdom of God (ch. 1:24) defines the content of the wisdom imparted by the Holy Spirit (ch. 2:10). It is that wisdom which is to be identified with the hearing of the living Christ afresh in each new situation — that hearing of the truth as an event which comes of the fact that where the Spirit is, there Christ is, and where Christ is, there the gospel is. In other words, a man of faith is not one who hears the gospel only once and thereafter deduces certain propositions from it which he applies to life, as if these propositions of themselves were equivalent to the wisdom of the Spirit. Such a substitution of theology for Christ ignores the fact that a man of faith is one who hears the gospel repeatedly because he hears Christ repeatedly in living fellowship with him — albeit the gospel in its rich variety of form and relevance. In this respect such hearing of Christ as the wisdom of God is equivalent to revelation. (4) It is less likely that Paul would conceive of the wisdom imparted by the Holy Spirit as equivalent to propositional or doctrinal truth, because this would provide no adequate answer to the problem of idolatrous loyalties. His recognition of the depth of this problem — the necessity of a fundamental change of heart as a consequence of revelation — would forbid the assumption that a better knowledge of theology could correct these loyalties. Such wisdom as theology represents in its primary function as the interpretation of revelation possesses validity only in the living, personal context of revelation as the original wisdom. It is the latter with which Paul is presently more concerned — the wisdom that changes the heart, as ch. 2:9-10 indicates.

If we assume, then, that the gospel is the hidden wisdom of God, which the mature hear as revelation through the action of the Holy Spirit — an action that in fact has made them mature — it follows that the babes in Christ hear the gospel after a fashion and yet do not hear it. They hear a form of it and are attracted by it but do not hear its essential, living content, Christ himself as identical with the graciousness (grace) of God. In this respect they fail to hear it for the same reason that " the word of the cross is folly to those who are perishing " (ch. 1:18) — not because it is a mystery hidden as the unknown from the ignorant or as the esoteric from the uninitiated, but as divine love from human pride. They fail to hear it for essentially the same reason that God in Christ was hidden from those who in putting him to death could think of him only as a criminal (cf. ch. 2:8). They are so confident they know what God is like that their confidence becomes the greatest obstacle in the way of their knowing him. To express this idea in another form, worldly wisdom, with its self-defined, self-possessed knowledge of God, comprising all the standards of spirituality and of divinity devised by men — standards that are but various measuring sticks in their hands — is characterized by one thing: it is unable to recognize that what ultimately matters is a knowledge of God that can be accepted only as a gift and, equally important, enjoyed only in its continuance as a gift.

The importance of such recognition is signified in Paul's quotation of the unidentifiable Scriptural source on the hidden character of the divine wisdom that has been imparted (ch. 2:9). The quotation is unexcelled as a means of indicating that such wisdom comes to man only as a gift and therefore as revelation. " What God has prepared for those who love him " — presumably their salvation — " no eye has seen, nor ear heard, nor the heart of man conceived." This wisdom is not such that a man can say: "I have already seen or heard that. I thought of it first. I do not need to be told it," and therefore can listen to God as if already knowing he needs to know only a little more or needs merely to have his knowledge confirmed. For this would be the opposite of receiving it solely as a gift and therefore with that joy and surprise typical of a child who receives something of which he was unaware and could not conceive. There would be nothing essentially new about it, only more of the old added to the old (cf. Mark 2:21-22; II Cor. 5:17).

Even atheists presume to possess a knowledge of God of this description, since they are as confident as anyone else of what God would be like or what he would do if he existed. Their denial of his existence should not obscure the standards or basic postulates by means of which they select or reject the supposed evidence out of which their negative conclusion emerges. Their peculiar situation is such that by their knowledge of God they deny his existence, which of course, is not so different from the action of those who, when he appeared among them, sought to destroy him. For on the basis of their knowledge of him, the atheists also think of him as a criminal — as one inimical to the best interests of society as they conceive it. Yet, apart from their negative reaction, they bear a striking resemblance to the conventionally religious man in that their rigidly confident knowledge of God is similar to his, when he presumes to know God with the facile understanding of a man who thinks he has all the answers.

It is such a presumptuous knowledge of God which the acceptance of God's wisdom as a gift invalidates. The wisdom which no eye has seen, nor ear heard, nor the heart of man conceived, which nevertheless, as Paul says, has been revealed (ch. 2:10) — and this to the mature — enables the recipient to abandon all his measuring sticks of God. He stands before God as one who, in the words of the hymn, confesses, "Nothing in my hand I bring, simply to thy cross I cling," [8] and who is humbled by the wonder that belongs to faith. He realizes

what it means to exclaim, " Who has known the mind of the
Lord, or who has been his counselor? " (Rom. 11:34). In this
respect his attitude bears a certain resemblance to agnosticism.
But his abandonment of his measuring sticks in a willingness to
accept his knowledge of God as a gift is as different from agnosticism as day is from night, because it is essentially a manifestation of the childlike spirit necessary for entrance into the
Kingdom of Heaven (Matt. 18:3; Mark 10:15; Luke 18:17).

By means of such a spirit, valid loyalties are established, because the man who has abandoned his measuring sticks of God
will abandon his measuring sticks of his brother; his surrender
of his rigid, judgmental attitude toward God will be accompanied by the surrender of a similar attitude toward his brother.
He will not label or categorize his brother or refuse to change
his opinion of him for better or worse. Nor will he exalt his
brother to idolatrous heights or damn him to demonic depths
and thus create dissensions in the church and the society. Instead, he will accept his brother as a gift, as he accepts his
knowledge of God as a gift, and therefore as the opposite of a
possession he has the right to appropriate. This will mean the
end of the acquisitive spirit that prompts a congregation to
assume that Paul, Apollos, Cephas, or their modern equivalents
are their men, belonging to them as heroes, personalities, or
employees. For it should be recognized that there is an affinity
between this acquisitive spirit and the readiness to make much
of a spiritual leader which is but the failure to recognize that
the ministry is the gift of God.

The revelation of that which no eye has seen nor ear heard
nor the heart of man conceived — that which God has prepared for those who love him — is not the communication of
a quantum of knowledge that can be added to a stock of
knowledge already possessed, because this would mean the
transformation of a gift into a possession and therefore into
something subject to man's control and manipulation. Instead
it is a searching of everything — the depths of the human heart
and even the depths of God — not for the purpose of discover-
ing more knowledge as a possession, but knowledge in its

personal connotation. The best analogy would be that of the lover knowing the beloved — active as love gives of itself and finds response in the beloved who also gives. In this respect it is an activity equivalent to the birth of love within the human heart in response to the previous gift of God (cf. I John 4:7-10, 19). The heart may be understood here as the integrative center of the individual's life, the secret source of his motivation where all his loyalties find their origin and sustenance.

Described in this manner, revelation may seem to be only the Biblical equivalent of a deep, psychical process known to some as " individuation," on the basis of which a new knowledge of the self is acquired.[9] It may appear to be only the voice of the human unconscious heard as if its projected form came from beyond as the word of God — as if the searching or the peculiar activity were " other " than that natural to the human psyche. Over against such a psychological denial of the transcendence of revelation, Paul's characteristic consistency in maintaining a sharp line between God and man should not be regarded as religious naiveté, as if God were only the projected image of the human psyche. Transcendence in its evangelical connotation cannot be explained away in such a facile manner, if for no other reason than the fact that it still leaves the psychologist with the kind of desperate, unresolved human problem depicted in Sartre's *No Exit*.[10] Individuation, with its implicit naturalism, is no answer to the problem of objective guilt when there is no way out — no beyond, no justice, nothing other than people with the same problem, who, as Sartre sees, are themselves definitive of hell without fire and brimstone, and even without a devil. As each character in this well-known play attempts to find in the other the answer for his deepest need (cf. idolatrous loyalty) and only finds the problem he knows too well within himself, he turns against him, making fellowship impossible because of endless discord (cf. dissensions). The problem of guilt as thus described cannot be outgrown or left behind as individuation implies, nor absolved even by death, because if there be no God or no real (objective) forgiveness commensurate with the objectivity of such guilt, man is shut up unto himself. The only hope in this case is from beyond — is the genuine action of God, which breaks through the imprisonment with a forgiveness as unique as God himself. As a consequence, it relieves men of seeking in one another what they can find only in God, and thus of the need of idolizing another either as a personality or as a collective.

It is this transcendence which may be inferred from the significant word: " For what person knows a man's thoughts except the spirit of the man which is in him? So also no one comprehends the thoughts of God except the Spirit of God " (v. 11). Such revelation is the freedom of God to be himself in the heart of man, which, strangely enough, frees the man to be himself. It is God thinking his thoughts in the heart of man — knowing himself by means of himself, which on the analogy of solipsism is only Paul's attempt to express as well as he can the epistemological corollary of *sola gratia*. For a man to come to the end of himself, so that now he is able to accept not only his life and destiny but his knowledge of God as a gift, frees him from that strange necessity, that inner restlessness and feeling of inadequacy, which prompts him to say, " I'm for Paul, I'm for Apollos, I'm for Cephas." For now he has taken to heart the truth of the words: " What have you that you did not receive? If then you received it, why do you boast as if it were not a gift? " (ch. 4:7).

As if to reemphasize the secret by means of which they understand the gifts bestowed upon them by God, Paul affirms in ch. 2:12, " Now we have received not the spirit of the world, but the Spirit which is from God." The God who gives of himself in the crucified Christ is the one whose presence enables a man to understand what has really been given to him and therefore to accept his life with gratitude. This gratitude, which is correlative with what God has given, is essentially a new self-knowledge as it is also a new knowledge of others. This was implied in the previous reference to the acceptance of one's brother as a gift. At the same time it is the basis of communication with others, as Paul implies in the subsequent statement, " We impart this in words not taught by human wisdom but taught by the Spirit, interpreting spiritual truths to those who possess the Spirit " (v. 13). Having regard to the problem of loyalties that has exercised Paul's mind through the letter to this point, it seems natural to conclude that what he means here pertains less to abstract teaching than to interpersonal communication. Since the Spirit is the agent of the communication and associated with the wisdom previously equated with the gospel, the didactic character of the communication could be described as " didactic kerygma." But at no point would the didactic be subsequent to the kerygma, inasmuch as Christ is always present in the Spirit.[11] If not, the fellowship of believers (koinonia) would become more of an intellectual exchange than a genuine interpersonal communication. Although such an exchange should never be minimized as a highly essential component of the fellowship, it should not become the exclusive consideration that prevents communication from the personal depths of life, where, as Paul has previously said, the searching of the Holy Spirit is in evidence (cf. Heb. 4:12).

Paul says that, in contrast to the mature, " the unspiritual man does not receive the gifts of the Spirit of God, for they are folly to him, and he is not able to understand them because they are spiritually discerned " (ch. 2:14). The unspiritual man as a type would include both the babe in Christ within the church and the unbeliever outside the church. Both would have this in common, that the reception of the gifts of the Spirit would appear but a foolish possibility in comparison with the alleged realism of practical life. In the case of the babe in Christ, he fails to receive the wisdom of God as the gospel heard anew and related repeatedly to the great variety of human experience as revealed insight. Therefore, he is incapable of fellowship (koinonia), as Paul declares: " For while there is jealousy and strife among you, are you not of the flesh, and behaving like ordinary men? For when one says, ' I belong to Paul,' and another, ' I belong to Apollos,' are you not merely men? " (ch. 3:3-4). Thus neither the babe in Christ nor the unbeliever has had his soul searched by the

Spirit of God so that the arrogant center of judgment by which he appraises himself and others has been crucified with Christ and transformed. Neither has heard the gospel as revelation.

This is why neither is capable of the spiritual discernment of spiritual things (ch. 2:14b). For such discernment is not a religious version merely of the claim that only insiders are competent to judge a specific point of view and therefore those who in practice will be favorable to it. If this is what Paul meant by spiritual discernment of spiritual things, worldly wisdom could justify itself on a similar basis. The worst tyrant could claim that only insiders were capable of understanding the circumstances that made his action necessary. Instead, the spiritual discernment of which Paul speaks goes back to his claim that the knowledge of God can be received only as a gift. This at once distinguishes it from a point of view and therefore from a position only too ready to exploit the contextual argument of the favorable judgment of the insider. Spiritual discernment as a gift rather than as a position to be maintained is characterized as defenseless (cf. ch. 2:3-4). It is the weakness of God that is stronger than men. It pertains to the self-validating character of revelation, which neither imposes itself upon men nor defends itself, because its freedom is such that it never needs to fear. In this respect the spiritual man is free to judge all things, but is himself judged of no man (ch. 2:15). For what is judgment, if the judge be not really free? As one indwelt by the Spirit of God and therefore possessed of the mind of Christ, the spiritual man (mature) has that unique humility which is obedient even to the death of the cross (Phil. 2:5-11) because it is free from fear.

The problem that remains is how to distinguish somewhat more clearly the babe in Christ from the mature. This follows from Paul's explicit reference to the two categories at the beginning of the third chapter, in connection with idolatrous loyalties to himself and Apollos. The reference indicates that through the intervening section (chs. 1:18 to 2:16) the problem of loyalties has been his primary theme. To this point our conclusion has been that the difference between the two turns on the question of their receptivity of the wisdom of God and that, more specifically, this means the hearing of the gospel as revelation. In other words, the fundamental answer to the problem of idolatrous loyalties is revelation. It is revelation that is definitive of the mature. This, as we have seen, means that God has dealt with them at the judgmental center of their lives. But this statement has to be amplified. For it is important to recognize that in the letter to the Philippians, Paul indicates that maturity is not finally obtained until the resurrection of the dead (cf. Phil. 3:15 with ch. 3:12). This means that for him, in sharp contrast to modern developmental conceptions influenced by the biological sciences, maturity is an eschatological category. For this reason the term " mature," just as from another point of view the term " perfect," is an inadequate translation of what Paul means by *teleioi*. The important consideration which therefore emerges is that the resurrection of the dead, the theme of the fifteenth chapter of First Corinthians, constitutes Paul's elaborated answer, at the end of the letter, to the problem of idolatrous loyalties, which appears at the beginning. Resurrection as the definition of maturity provides the answer to the immaturity definitive of idolatrous loyalties. This means that for Paul the resurrection of the dead and revelation are essentially the same. The transformation that occurs at the judgmental center of a man's life by virtue of which he becomes mature is the resurrection already begun within him (cf. Rom. 8:11, 23).

But what of the babes in Christ? Are they not also believers? Are they not distinguished from the men of the world who reject the gospel? To each of these questions an affirmative answer must be given because the strange fact confronts us throughout that Paul never condemns the babes in Christ as apostate. He has sharp, frank words to say to them but he never denies that they are in Christ. They are all his children whom he has begotten through the gospel (I Cor. 4:15) and who are beloved of him (ch. 16:24). What, then, does he mean by "babes in Christ," and how does he distinguish them from unbelievers? The answer lies in his conception of God working in the life of a man prior to revelation and thereby disposing him to be attracted by the gospel and to the church. In this respect the answer is related to the way in which Paul views everything in the light of the election of God according to grace (cf. Gal. 1:15; Rom. 8:29-30; 9:10-18). Appealing again to a text from Philippians, the babe in Christ is one who has yet to work out his salvation in fear and trembling — that is to say, to become the recipient of God's revelation as that action which deals with him at the center of his life, as the remainder of the text so clearly states: " For God is at work in you, both to will and to work for his good pleasure " (Phil. 2:13). This should not be regarded as a concession to a developmental conception, because the working of God in the life of a man is characterized by a freedom that has its analogy in the resurrection of the dead rather than in the laws of growth. It always partakes of the offense of the cross and of *sola gratia*. Thus, we can reiterate that the babe in Christ has heard the gospel and yet not heard it. He has been attracted and involved — perhaps as one who for reasons he cannot understand is interested in the work of the church, as well as in its message and teaching, and perhaps as one who has entered its ministry. He may even be persuaded that salvation is entirely of grace and be deeply interested in theology and scholarship and in the practical work of the church, giving generously of his time and substance just as did those Corinthians whose alleged spiritual success Paul disclaimed as presumptuous (ch. 4:8). But he has not really heard the gospel and for this reason come to the end of himself — so that now being free from himself he might have that freedom which will permit him to become a servant of Christ.

VI

THE MINISTRY OF GRACE
3:5-15

3 *What then is Apollos? What is Paul? Servants through whom you believed, as the Lord assigned to each.* [6] *I planted, Apollos watered, but God gave the growth.* [7] *So neither he who plants nor he who waters is anything, but only God who gives the growth.* [8] *He who plants and he who waters are equal, and each shall receive his wages according to his labor.* [9] *For we are fellow workers for God; you are God's field, God's building.*

10 *According to the commission of God given to me, like a skilled master builder I laid a foundation, and another man is building upon it. Let each man take care how he builds upon it.* [11] *For no other foundation can any one lay than that which is laid, which is Jesus Christ.* [12] *Now if any one builds on the foundation with gold, silver, precious stones, wood, hay, stubble —* [13] *each man's work will become manifest; for the Day will disclose it, because it will be revealed with fire, and the fire will test what sort of work each one has done.* [14] *If the work which any man has built on the foundation survives, he will receive a reward.* [15] *If any man's work is burned up, he will suffer loss, though he himself will be saved, but only as through fire.*

It would seem that Paul's purpose in this section is to correct that erroneous conception of the ministry represented by the idolatrous loyalties. As in the previous section, in which he developed his normative conception of the wisdom of God, the emphasis throughout is positive and intimately related to his eschatological understanding of maturity. The latter serves to define the nature of the ministry and the quality of those eligible for it. It sets the limits within which the ministry fulfills its original purpose, in that the mature make the best ministers, whereas babes in Christ make the poorest — when from worldly wisdom the latter feel they are called to it.

The section begins with two strongly rhetorical questions: " What then is Apollos? What is Paul? " followed immediately by the answer: " Servants through whom you believed, as the Lord assigned to each " (v. 5). The description of the two men as servants sharply distinguishes their status from that of idols, which is presupposed by those who say, " I belong to Paul," or " I belong to Apollos." For a servant is sufficiently opposite to an idol, that it is always difficult to sustain an idolatrous loyalty toward him. For who feels puffed up over a servant? Who wishes to say to him, " I belong to you " when his servitude involves him in the offense of the cross?

In this, of course, as in all forms of servitude, the decisive consideration is what it specifically means. What particular task or function defines it? In what respect is the minister of Christ a servant? The answer that appears in the text is not the answer represented by the variety of duties expected of him by popular religion, which frequently makes his ministry so onerous and yet so futile. It is briefly indicated by the phrase " through whom you believe," which defines the locus of the servitude. A minister is one whose peculiar role as a servant makes him the means by which people come to a saving knowledge of Christ. As illustrated from the ministry of Paul, it concerns the fact that he became their spiritual father in Christ through the gospel (ch. 4:15). Even though it has to be distinguished somewhat sharply from the Socratic conception of the philosopher as a midwife and from the modern clinical conception of the therapist as a nondirective agent, it resembles both in its importance and uniqueness.[12] Although easily oversimplified and often vaguely misconstrued partly for lack of an adequate theology of evangelism, the minister's role constitutes a task of such magnitude and of such urgency that it is an incomparable challenge to the most devoted men.

As the human agent by means of which God creates faith in the heart of the believer, the minister is tempted to forget, however, that he is a servant and to begin priding himself on being a helper. For there is often an implicit pride in the thought that others have been the recipients of his helpfulness. Thus he begins by saying to himself: " This is partly my action. In a measure I am Lord. I am not entirely a servant." His piety, personality, and scholarship conspire against the call to servitude in the thought of doing what only God can do. If he yields, he becomes less a servant and more a master. If his people yield, they exalt him to a higher level than themselves in what amounts to an idolatrous relationship. Sensitivity to the ease with which this temptation confronts the servant of Christ may have been the reason that Paul appended the phrase " as the Lord assigned to each." Whether it means faith assigned to each believer or success to each servant, it is indicative of divine grace.

Paul acknowledges that he and Apollos have had a certain part in bringing about faith in the hearts of the Corinthians: " I planted, Apollos watered." But he is quick to declare that it has only been the part of servants, not of masters. The strongly adversative " but " in the succeeding clause — " but God gave the growth " — prepares the way for the sharp contrast he draws between himself and Apollos on the one hand and God on the other. It appears in the conclusion: " So neither he who plants nor he who waters is anything, but only God who gives the growth " (v. 7). The contrast between their achievement and that of God is clear. Neither has added anything to the action of God in the creation of faith. They have remained servants through it all. Their planting and watering are ordinary actions as compared to the ancient conception of growth as miraculous. Growth, as representative of God's action, distinguishes his action from theirs. The inference is that they are not possessed of a special grace or charismatic power by means of which they can add their miracle to God's. The idea that such grace or power could be conferred on them as a possession, to be manipulated and controlled by them, would have been only a subtler form of the temptation to supplement the action of God in the creation of faith. It would have been a sign of refusal to be a servant.

Neither Paul nor Apollos, therefore, has any advantage over the other. In relation to the achievement of God, " he who plants and he who waters are equal." For one to be puffed up in favor of himself over the other, as if he were better able to supplement the work of God, would have been absurd. There can be no question of supplementing the creation of faith when what God reveals " no eye has seen, nor ear heard, nor the heart of man conceived " — not even those of Paul and Apollos. In their reception of such revelation they are equally dependent and equally constituted as servants of God. They are not rivals but fellow workmen whose cooperative role in relation to one another is determined by the fact that they belong to God. The decisive fact is that they are possessed of him (cf. Gal. 1:15), as the ninth verse indicates by the emphatic position of the genitive *theou* and the parallel affirmative that the people are possessed of him as his field or building. They are not fellow workers with God, engaged in a synergistic cooperation with him, but fellow workers who belong to him. But in their servitude to him they are not exploited and treated as less than human, despite the fact that they add nothing to the achievement of God in the creation of faith. For the God to whom they belong is the God of grace who justly rewards his servants even though they have no claim upon his favor and no thought of a reward. " Each shall receive his wages according to his labor." The servant is not one whose role is symbolized by numerical zero.

Those who complain, however, that the role of a servant as thus defined does reduce the minister to the point where his role may be symbolized by numerical zero, as if a synergistic cooperation were the issue to be bitterly championed, forget that Paul's theology is eminently practical. The question is not a theoretical one, to be decided apart from the context of personal relationships and the ultimate meaning of helpfulness as experience defines it. For it not infrequently happens, if not always, that a minister who in the delicate matter of the searching of the heart and the birth of faith conceives of his role as that of a helper actually hinders his helpfulness. In this respect there is a peculiar parallel between Paul's insistence that, at the critical point of decision, the servant is not to conceive of himself as a helper, and the insistence of the psychotherapist that the role of helper must be rejected.[13] On this basis the conclusion that neither he who plants nor he who waters is anything, agrees with the peculiar neutrality of the therapist, which has the effect of encouraging the client to be free.

At this point in the section (ch. 3:10), Paul employs another metaphor — that of a foundation with its superstructure. As a skilled master builder he has laid the foundation. But since another man is building upon it, he is concerned for the quality of the superstructure — that it be worthy of the foundation on which it is erected. His concern comes out clearly in his exhortation, "Let each man take care how he builds upon it." The problem is not that of the relation between himself and his successors, as it would at first seem to be. It is the relation between the foundation established of God in the hearts of his people through Paul's preaching, and his successors, who began with this fact and built upon it. It was not Paul's foundation, as if his successors were building upon him, nor was the problem one of a simple relationship between his work and theirs. It was Christ's foundation appropriated in the faith event. In the previous metaphor the planting and watering were anterior to the work of God in giving the growth (ch. 3:7). But in the present metaphor the erection of the superstructure is subsequent to the work of God in establishing the foundation. The previous metaphor therefore has reference to the preaching ministry, the latter to the pastoral ministry. But the problem is essentially the same — the relation between the work of God and the work of man, the latter being the work of servants.

Since we have already seen what it means to be a servant in

the preaching ministry, we have now to see what it means in the pastoral ministry. To do this we have to recognize that when Paul exhorted his successors to take care how they built upon the event of faith in Christ, he meant their utter dependence upon this foundation. It was a foundation worthy of the finest superstructure as a testimony to its supporting power. This is why anyone who builds on the foundation with gold, silver, or precious stones testifies, through the quality of his pastoral work, to the saving power of Christ, whereas anyone who builds upon it with wood, hay, or stubble makes mockery of it. In fact, the latter bears a certain resemblance to the antinomian contempt for grace which would let the foundation erect its own superstructure.

There is no place in the metaphor for the superstructure as a supplement to the foundation according to the claim that the work of God requires the work of man for its completion. For this would mean that the pastor was not respecting the work of Christ as the foundation on which at all times he must depend. It would also be a denial that the claim of the previous metaphor applies equally to the pastor, and that he also is a servant. For when Paul uses his architectural metaphor he is really speaking of the living, personal relationship between pastors and Christ, for which the metaphor, in the strictest sense, is inadequate. In this context the role of the pastor as a servant presupposes a dependency upon the foundation comparable to the dependency upon the divinely given growth in the metaphor of planting and watering.

This is not a dependency in the form of a rigid, arbitrary adherence to a doctrine as the firm foundation of faith but the locus of personal trust and the practice of always encouraging the people to throw themselves back upon it. Instead of the pastor's encouraging them to trust in him in an idolatrous fashion, or throwing them back upon themselves as if their human resources were adequate to resolve the guilt of sin or the enigma of death, he throws them back upon the crucified Christ. This is not simply a matter of exhortation, with a stereotyped appeal to the same words and phrases and the same

Scriptural texts. It is that of assisting a believer to rediscover in each new experience what it means to put his ultimate trust in the crucified Savior. For although faith possesses a " onceness " symbolized by the one foundation and the unrepeatability of baptism, it would be erroneous to assume, as often is done, that the believer needs to hear the gospel only once, and afterward only its interpretation. The dependence upon Christ the foundation is not a dependence solely upon a past event but upon a person who is the same yesterday, today, and forever. He is living, and his gospel is living and has to be heard anew in each situation in which the believer finds himself. Although the believer has heard the gospel, he will have to learn anew what it means, in failure as in success, in sickness as in health, in bereavement as in the joy of daily life. Pastoral work is the fellowship of one believer with another for this purpose. It is a form of interpretation which is inseparable from testimony by word and deed. In this context all the problems and crises peculiar to a human being will come under the purview of the pastor. But the therapeutic center of reference will be different from that of the modern clinician.

Consequently, the task of the pastor is to minister to the eschatological maturity of his people. In this respect the concept of maturity is corporate as well as individual, involving the whole church in its understanding of what is really involved in the creation of koinonia (fellowship). While it includes the didactic, it is inseparable from the believer's living relationship with Christ, and integral always to the ethical life and practice of the church. Qualified in such a manner, the relation between pastoral work and the event of faith pertains to the future as well as to the past. Christ the foundation is not only past and present but future, and the dependency upon him reflects this fact. This is why a narrowly chronological interpretation of pastoral work as being subsequent to the event of faith is inadequate. It follows too literally the fact that the superstructure is subsequent to the foundation in the strictest sense. But in Paul's metaphor of the superstructure he moves to the point of its testing in the Day of the Lord, in which the quality of every man's work will be manifest. " The fire will test what sort of work each one has done." (V. 13.) The question of dependency implicit in this judgment derives from the Christological nature of the norm of judgment. Although Paul does not say as much in this instance, his references elsewhere to a similar judgment are sufficiently Christological that they warrant our assuming it here. In the eschatological end the test of the work of every pastor will be the quality of its dependence upon Christ in every respect, which will mean the test of dependence upon his grace. Paul does not go so far as to say that the poor work of a pastor could undo the grace of Christ, because this would represent in a negative manner the work of man as determining the work of God. One who insisted that " where sin increased, grace abounded all the more " could hardly sanction such a possibility. Yet he did insist that a pastor of this description would be saved only by the narrowest margin: " He will suffer loss, though he himself will be saved, but only as through fire " (v. 15).

VII

THE INTEGRITY OF THE MINISTRY
4:1-13

4 *This is how one should regard us, as servants of Christ and stewards of the mysteries of God. ² Moreover it is required of stewards that they be found trustworthy. ³ But with me it is a very small thing that I should be judged by you or by any human court. I do not even judge myself. ⁴ I am not aware of anything against myself, but I am not thereby acquitted. It is the Lord who judges me. ⁵ Therefore do not pronounce judgment before the time, before the Lord comes, who will bring to light the things now hidden in darkness and will disclose the purposes of the heart. Then every man will receive his commendation from God.*

6 I have applied all this to myself and Apollos for your benefit, brethren, that you may learn by us to live according to scripture, that none of you may be puffed up in favor of one against another. ⁷ For who sees anything different in you? What have you that you did not receive? If then you received it, why do you boast as if it were not a gift?

8 Already you are filled! Already you have become rich! Without us you have become kings! And would that you did reign, so that we might share the rule with you! ⁹ For I think that God has exhibited us apostles as last of all, like men sentenced to death; because we have become a spectacle to the world, to angels and to men. ¹⁰ We are fools for Christ's sake, but you are wise in Christ. We are weak, but you are strong. You are held in honor, but we in disrepute. ¹¹ To the present hour we hunger and thirst, we are ill-clad and buffeted and homeless, ¹² and we labor, working with our own hands. When reviled, we bless; when persecuted, we endure;

[13] *when slandered, we try to conciliate; we have become, and are now, as the refuse of the world, the offscouring of all things.*

When Paul warned of the destruction of the temple of God, which he identified with the Corinthians as a people indwelt of the Holy Spirit, he seems to have had one or several persons in mind (ch. 3:16-17). His use of the singular in v. 17, "If any one destroys God's temple, God will destroy him," and similarly v. 18, "If any one among you thinks he is wise," leaves this impression. When taken with the reference to those arrogant persons whose empty talk he proposes to put to the test on his arrival (ch. 4:18-19), the suspicion is confirmed. Although he does not name them, he has probably had them in mind in all that he has previously said of the idolatrous loyalties. The fact that "they had plans and a concerted purpose is put beyond doubt by [his] subsequent attack on their adroit, subtle methods " [14] (II Cor. 4:2).

In their threat to the existence of the church these deceptive persons illustrate the strange manner in which a malignant spirit can infiltrate the ministry. Intent upon the exploitation of the popular tendency toward idolatrous loyalties, they were a menace to the best achievements of Paul and his fellow apostles. The danger seemed not unlike that so vividly described by Luther in his commentary on Galatians: " A man may labor half a score of years ere he build up some little church to be rightly and religiously ordered; and when it is so ordered there creepeth in some mad brain, yea, a very unlearned idiot . . . and he in one moment overthroweth it all." [15]

With a painful awareness of this possibility in Corinth, where from later material we learn of those whom Paul describes as servants of Satan (II Cor. 11:15), Paul's thoughts only naturally turned to the integrity which properly belongs to the ministry. Integrity would undoubtedly be the quality he would covet as much for the congregation as for the ministry, when he saw the people led by men whose falsity should have been transparent to them. This is why he emphasized

that the Corinthians should regard him and his fellow apostles
" as servants of Christ and stewards of the mysteries of God."
The church, as well as its ministry, must recognize that servants and stewards honor their Lord only by their acceptance
of responsibility for work well done in obedience to him. Since
Paul had previously indicated the definitive character of a
servant as one who in comparison to his Lord claims nothing
for himself (I Cor. 3:5-7), he probably feels that it is necessary to add only that the indispensable quality of a steward is
trustworthiness (ch. 4:2).

The meaning of such a quality in relation to the mysteries
of God will be evident from our equation of these mysteries
with the gospel. The reasons for such an equation are substan-
tially those adduced for the equation of the secret and hidden
wisdom of God with the gospel, supplemented by a preference for " mystery " instead of " testimony " as that which
Paul preached to the Corinthians (ch. 2:1). The plural form,
" mysteries of God," is probably determined by the associated
plurality of stores and treasures that a steward administers.
Their possible identity as truths of the gospel would not
empty them of kerygmatic content. Nor would it be proper to
exclude the sacraments as the cultic form of the gospel.

On this basis we can say that a trustworthy steward of the
mysteries of God is one who is faithful to the gospel regardless of consequences. As an indication of what this means,
Paul's attestation of his integrity and that of his fellow workers in II Cor. 4:2 is sufficiently clear: " We have renounced
disgraceful, underhanded ways; we refuse to practice cunning
or to tamper with God's word, but by the open statement of
the truth we would commend ourselves to every man's conscience in the sight of God." A clearer indication appears in
Paul's declared objective that in preaching to the Corinthians
he decided to know nothing among them except Jesus Christ
and him crucified (I Cor. 2:2). The integrity of the preacher
is defined by this one, exclusive purpose. Similarly in the succeeding chapter the pastor is to build carefully on the only
foundation that can be laid, which is Jesus Christ (ch. 3:11).

The conclusion that follows is that the integrity of the ministry of which Paul speaks must be understood as possessing an evangelical rather than a moral connotation. It is not merely dependability and consistency and other similar qualities as components of an integrity that characterizes the good man as such, or in another respect the socially acceptable man. It is rather the singleness of purpose, the obedience and diligence, the willingness to give of oneself, which derive from an unconditional, personal response to revelation, and this expressed with no profounder joy than in the communication of the gospel. It means the awareness of vocation as a separation unto the gospel and unto nothing else but the gospel.

As exemplified in Paul's attitude toward the judgments of the Corinthians, it can be said that such integrity concerns the freedom a minister has in Christ. The various dimensions of such freedom are evident from Paul's significant words: " But with me it is a very small thing that I should be judged by you or by any human court. I do not even judge myself. I am not aware of anything against myself, but I am not thereby acquitted. It is the Lord who judges me " (ch. 4:3-5). In this statement there is a freedom from others and a freedom from himself, derived from the freedom he finds only in his Lord.

The first has reference to the freedom to live without fear of the thoughts, words, or actions of others, and even of the formal action of a court of law. It is the freedom from that sensitivity to the opinions of others which would have made him their slave. In this respect Paul's example is more significant as we remember the variety and complexity of the trouble that confronted him and that was enough to try the best of men. Because Paul was comparatively alone in the early history of the church, without the resources which in subsequent times have often supported men in similar situations, his freedom was amazing. Some persons were boasting of him, others boasting of Apollos or Cephas. Nevertheless he was steadfast — neither flattered by the fact that some were for him, nor depressed by the fact that others were against him. It was not, for him, a question of personal prestige, since he was concerned about neither his importance nor his unimportance. The voice of popularity was not his god. He was not enslaved by all those subtle ways by which modern men are persuaded to follow the crowd in what they think or buy. Unlike those who continually inquire: " How do I look? How did I do? What will they think? " Paul had learned to be himself, and with this he had acquired the freedom to exercise his ministry.

In explaining such an achievement it is important to recognize Paul's freedom from his judgments of himself, or from what is probably better described as the tyranny of self-judgment. This is evident from his statement: " I do not even judge myself. I am not aware of anything against myself, but I am not thereby acquitted." It indicates that the probable reason why he was not caught up in the outward bondage was that he was not caught up in the inward bondage. He had no inward compulsion to have his opinions confirmed by others for the preservation of his self-esteem. Unlike those who without the slightest hesitation judge themselves superior or inferior, successful or unsuccessful, or who feel they are either indispensable to the world or worthless, Paul did not set himself up as the judge of his life and in this way usurp the prerogative of God. Although he was capable of self-criticism, he was free from that rigidity of judgment toward himself which is indicative of inward tyranny.

The real explanation of Paul's freedom from the judgments of others and from self-judgment is to be found in the knowledge that the Lord was his judge — the Lord who should come and who was therefore the Christ whom he loved and served (ch. 4:4). This Lord, whom he had thought was against him, was for him. He was a judge who judged him not to condemn him but to save him, not to reject him but to accept him. It was a strange judgment, which instead of convicting and sentencing him had acquitted and set him free, as we see from the significant text, " There is therefore now no condemnation for those who are in Christ Jesus " (Rom. 8:1). To see the consequences of such grace in Paul's personal life it is important to recognize not only his freedom from judgment in ch. 4:3 but his humility in ch. 3:7, where as a servant of the Lord he claims nothing for himself. For the same reason it is important to recognize his reception of revelation in ch. 2:9-10, where with the mature he accepts his knowledge of the Lord as a gift. All of these texts are really referring to the same consequence of grace (justification). They are indispensable for the light they throw upon the judgment of Christ as the means of freeing a man from the inward tyranny of a self-defined, self-possessed knowledge of God and, as we now can add, a similar self-defined, self-possessed knowledge of himself. Paul could hardly have said to the Corinthians, " I do not even judge myself," unless he had also said of himself in comparison to his Lord, " He who plants is nothing," and acknowledged that in his heart he had not conceived what God had prepared for those who love him. This, as previously indicated, is not to be confused with the ontological reduction of man to zero, which would be a form of annihilation inconsistent with divine love and the creation of personal freedom. It concerns instead the freeing of a man from himself, so that now he can be himself, serve others, and have the integrity necessary for the ministry. It is essentially the creation of the ability to receive (*analogia fidei*) the gift of God, by virtue of which a man is able to receive others as a gift, and most significantly, his own life. The integrity of the ministry is therefore essentially that self-knowledge which is correlative with *sola gratia*.

Paul sees all this in the context of the eschatological, as we see from his normative statement in ch. 4:5: " Therefore do not pronounce judgment before the time, before the Lord comes, who will bring to light things now hidden in darkness and will disclose the purposes of the heart. Then every man will receive his commendation from God." This Lord, as we have already indicated, was Jesus Christ, whom Paul affirms will be the one before whose judgment seat all must appear at the end of the age (II Cor. 5:10; Rom. 2:16). This is why he cautions against present judgments.

Present judgments should at best be only provisional, because no man is qualified to be the judge of others or of himself with the ultimate truth of eschatological judgment. Refraining from judgment as Paul recommends is therefore evidence of freedom from judgment out of a respect for such truth. It is a sign of integrity. It means that the man who refrains is open to the truth about himself and others no matter what his present provisional judgments might be. He leaves the final analysis of himself and others to Christ.

But if it were only a matter of leaving the prerogative of judgment to Christ, it could be only a freedom that was negative. It could be only a freedom that was irresponsibly inactive, always pleading with others never to judge and therefore always in the position of doing nothing. As such, it would be a menace to the integrity of the ministry. It would not have expressed that confidence of Paul in the judgment of Christ which was at the same time a tremendous consciousness of destiny. For Paul did not fear the judgment of Christ; he pressed forward to it (Phil. 3:14). He felt he was profoundly involved in it as a comprehensive judgment of the whole world, carrying him forward to its consummation (I Cor. 15:24-28). His whole ministry was understood in this eschatological context. Every problem that confronted him in the Corinthian church was seen in the light of it. His conception of it was so positive that he could say in the letter to the Romans, " I consider that the sufferings of this present time are not worth comparing with the glory that is to be revealed to us " (Rom. 8:18). He could express a similar confidence in Second Corinthians: " So we do not lose heart. Though our outer nature is wasting away, our inner nature is being renewed every day. For this slight momentary affliction is preparing for us an eternal weight of glory beyond all comparison " (II Cor. 4:16-17).

The importance of these observations on Paul's normative conception of eschatological judgment is reflected in his attitude toward the present, particularly in relation to hardship and suffering. His profound consciousness of destiny, his confidence that nothing could defeat the faith he proclaimed, remind one of a similar consciousness among those of the present age who feel that the ultimate victory of the revolutionary cause they espouse is given in the dialectical processes of history. For Paul it was not the dialectical processes of history but the redemptive purpose of God in Christ that could not be defeated. In this purpose it was his glorious privilege to participate.

This was why he and his fellow apostles could endure the hardship and suffering described in I Cor. 4:10-13, including the reputation of being the refuse of the world and the offscouring of all things. They could not have endured without being crushed in spirit or embittered and angered at life unless they had been inspired by a zeal and a purpose so powerful that it would more than compensate for it. Men have been frequently embittered and angered at life for less, indeed aroused to the point of murderous intent over matters relatively trivial. The degree of sensitivity they exhibit to any unfavorable reflections upon their status or privilege is often phenomenal. The slightest discomfort or the least failure to respect their wishes is often exaggerated out of all proportion to what it actually is. Consequently, when we consider what Paul and his fellow apostles suffered with a completely opposite effect, so that when reviled they blessed, when persecuted they endured, when slandered they tried to conciliate, we know the reason. It was their possession of a remarkable integrity, which in the midst of tribulation meant that they were free, and capable of such interest in life and of such appreciation of the ultimate purpose of their work that they found the greatest joy and satisfaction. They were effectively motivated by their eschatological outlook on life, by their Christological consciousness of destiny.

In contrast to such integrity it would seem that the conception of spiritual success which, according to Paul's satire (ch. 4:8), motivated the Corinthian church, or a significant portion of its membership, derived from a certain absolutizing of the present. For this reason it would be inconsistent with the eschatological outlook that characterized his ministry. Those of whom he could say: " Already you are filled! Already you have become rich! Without us you have become kings! " had arrived at the goal of destiny, so to speak. They had found in the present a substitute for what Paul and his fellow apostles had anticipated only at the end, in the resurrection of the dead. There was therefore no straining forward to what lay ahead, no pressing " toward the goal for the prize of the upward call of God in Christ Jesus " (Phil. 3:14). They were too obsessed with the present for such an orientation to the future.

In the absolutizing of the present, illustrated by a loyalty both to ministers and to the institutional church that tends to become a substitute for an overarching awareness of destiny, indeed for the hope of the resurrection, integrity is destroyed. Since loyalty to the church tends to be substituted for loyalty to Christ, the ministry loses its freedom to the extent that the claim of such a church becomes a total claim. As the people depend more upon the minister for the success of the church, always looking for the perfect man (idol), and as he depends more upon them for his self-appraisal and more upon their reaction as the validation of his message, the integrity of both deteriorates, because Christ is crowded out. Neither is free enough from the other to be free for one another. Their mutual dependency is of such a nature that it prevents their coming to the maturity of those who see that such dependency is but sinking sand compared to the foundation that is laid in Jesus Christ, of which the resurrection of the dead is the completed superstructure.

In contrast to such dependency, the integrity of Paul in its ethical expression was just as seriously and positively motivated as its evangelical expression. The eschatological hope inspired present ethical action and gave it a validity it would not otherwise have received. The tremendous awareness of destiny was a stimulus not to grow weary in well-doing (Gal. 6:9). In this way the ethical was liberated from those circumstances of mutual dependency of church and minister which tend to equate it with social approval or disapproval. The good was not, therefore, something done only to be seen of men. Nor was it done to claim the favor of God, since already in Christ the believer had been accepted of him and freed from condemnation. It was rather of the nature of a witness out of the spontaneous desire that all should share in the glory to be finally revealed at the end of the age (Rom. 8:18). In this respect it resembled the sacrificial goodness of a revolutionary zeal that finds its satisfaction in the confidence of ultimate victory.

For this reason neither Paul nor his fellow apostles seemed to have suffered from loneliness or from a feeling of isolation and helplessness, despite the fact they were such a minority and without the resources so often regarded as indispensable to the life and work of the church. Although there were no preestablished congregations or administrative structures of security that would provide a base of operations for their ministry, this did not destroy their morale. The possibility of loneliness seems to have been dispelled by a tremendous sense of urgency dictated by an awareness of the brevity of the time at the disposal of their ministry.

VIII

THE FAILURE OF DISCIPLINE
5:1-8; 6:1-8

5 *It is actually reported that there is immorality among you, and of a kind that is not found even among pagans; for a man is living with his father's wife.* ² *And you are arrogant! Ought you not rather to mourn? Let him who has done this be removed from among you.*

3 *For though absent in body I am present in spirit, and as if present, I have already pronounced judgment* ⁴ *in the name of the Lord Jesus on the man who has done such a thing. When you are assembled, and my spirit is present, with the power of our Lord Jesus,* ⁵ *you are to deliver this man to Satan for the destruction of the flesh, that his spirit may be saved in the day of the Lord Jesus.*

6 *Your boasting is not good. Do you not know that a little leaven leavens the whole lump?* ⁷ *Cleanse out the old leaven that you may be a new lump, as you really are unleavened. For Christ, our paschal lamb, has been sacrificed.* ⁸ *Let us, therefore, celebrate the festival, not with the old leaven, the leaven of malice and evil, but with the unleavened bread of sincerity and truth.*

6 *When one of you has a grievance against a brother, does he dare go to law before the unrighteous instead of the saints?* ² *Do you not know that the saints will judge the world? And if the world is to be judged by you, are you incompetent to try trivial cases?* ³ *Do you not know that we are to judge angels? How much more, matters pertaining to this life!* ⁴ *If then you have such cases, why do you lay them before those who are least esteemed by the church?* ⁵ *I say this to your shame. Can it be that there is no man*

among you wise enough to decide between members of the brotherhood, 6 *but brother goes to law against brother, and that before unbelievers?*

7 *To have lawsuits at all with one another is defeat for you. Why not rather suffer wrong? Why not rather be defrauded?* 8 *But you yourselves wrong and defraud, and that even your own brethren.*

After the long, substantial treatment of the idolatrous loyalties in the Corinthian church, Paul turns his attention to an urgent problem of discipline. A member of the church is guilty of incest — a form of immorality of such gravity that it would not be found even among pagans. It was a man living with his father's wife — probably a widowed stepmother or concubine — which in spite of the moral laxity of Greco-Roman city life was considered most offensive. Equally disturbing, or more so, was the complacency of the church, which had done nothing to correct the scandal. Its members were arrogant in their spirituality and had no sensitivity to the manner in which such immorality reflected unfavorably upon them. Instead of mourning at the thought of it, they were as convinced as ever of the high quality of their religious life and had no inclination to act.

This man was not the only problem character with whom the apostle had had to contend. In an earlier letter he had warned the Corinthians of associating with immoral men — surprisingly enough within the church — men guilty of immorality, greed, idolatry, abusive language, drunkenness, and robbery (ch. 5:9-11). Consistent with this fact, he acknowledges in the present letter that some of those now baptized, consecrated, and justified had been guilty of similar sins (ch. 6:9-11). The total impression is undoubtedly disturbing to modern conventional standards of church membership. For these queer saints of Corinth resemble recruits from the underworld or from the spiritual no-man's-land of beatniks or perverts who might well adorn the pages of a Dostoevsky novel. Their peculiarity confirms the literal character of Paul's description of the church as largely composed of the foolish and weak, the low and despised (ch. 1:27-28).

For those pagans who were sensitive to the gravity of incest, such an impression of the church would not be inconsistent with the scandal that had now arisen within it. A religion that had attracted such people would undoubtedly be under suspicion. When it failed to react with the same seriousness as the more responsible portion of pagan society, it would be under additional suspicion. With its leaders impugned as the refuse of the world and the offscouring of all things (ch. 4:13), the conclusion would inevitably follow that such scandal was no surprise.

On the contrary, Paul's reaction was quick and decisive. In this respect he seems to have stood virtually alone between a weak church and a pagan world. As one who in such a situation refused to compromise, and whose list of those excluded from the Kingdom of God (ch. 6:9-10) covered all categories of the unrighteous against whom he had warned (ch. 5:11) and from which some had been saved (ch. 6:11), he called for the expulsion of the incestuous man. His call, which constitutes the theme of the fifth chapter, and is repeated in several forms for emphasis, urged the Corinthians to remove him (v. 2), deliver him to Satan (v. 5), clean house of his evil influence (v. 7), not even to eat with him (v. 11), and indeed to drive him out (v. 13).

The sharpness of Paul's demand in what is almost a crescendo of intolerance will undoubtedly shock the modern Christian unaccustomed to the thought of expelling anyone from the church. It will savor of an arbitrary spirit that is quick to discipline but slower to understand, and for this reason less acceptable to an enlightened age. From the point of view of a so-called gospel of success, the incestuous conduct of the man would probably be regarded as sickness rather than sin. Or if it was regarded as sin, it would be a sin amenable to such a gospel as the alleged solution of every problem of faith and life in an almost magical manner. Rather than admit the reality of hardened characters whose perversion defies faith and whose obduracy is better known to the legal profession, the police, and social agencies, such a gospel of success prefers to minimize sin. Theoretically, this gospel holds that every problem character can be saved by a thorough effort over a sufficient period of time. On this basis the incestuous man should be permitted to remain indefinitely within the church. The hope of some benefit accruing to him by his continued presence should never be lost. One should never give up seeking to influence him.

The Corinthian church was similarly complacent — whatever may have been the distortion of the gospel that accounted for its inaction. According to Paul, its complacency was associated with pride and arrogance (ch. 5:2), which are probably the best words to describe the presupposition that no sin is ever sufficiently serious nor any case ever so hopeless that the sinner should be expelled from the church. The complacency of the Corinthians may be very well explained on this basis, which is simply the equivalent of a high confidence in their religious success. For why should those who were convinced they were spiritually filled and rich, and reigning as kings (ch. 4:8), fear the presence of one incestuous man in their midst? How could he harm them when they were so clearly delivered from the sin that enslaved him? The important consideration would be their influence upon him, and not his upon them. It was therefore desirable that he remain in the church as long as possible in order that eventually he might be changed for the better through them.

If this be an approximate interpretation of the pride and the arrogance which accounted for the dubious tolerance of the Corinthians toward the incestuous man, we can see how any gospel of success, ancient or modern, creates a serious problem of discipline within the church. For it is not unlike the self-confident spirituality that depends upon praying without acting, upon the efficacy of its moral and social example without involvement, upon love without the necessity of law, upon worship without mission and genuine outreach. The complacency which in Corinth was consistent with such quietism was equally consistent with the corruption of social life and the sexual adventures within the Christian community. In this respect it was not so different from the depravity of conscience evident in the various problem characters with whom Paul had to contend. The church's complacency was a sign of deep inward involvement in a religious form of decadence and therefore was indicative of the extent of the problem of discipline.

Under these circumstances Paul seems to have acted as if he were the conscience of the Corinthian church, out of a loving identification with them (cf. ch. 4:14-16) rather than a desire to impose his will upon them. Although absent from Corinth, he pronounced judgment on the guilty man and called upon the congregation to expel him: "When you are assembled, and my spirit is present, with the power of our Lord Jesus, you are to deliver this man to Satan for the destruction of the flesh, that his spirit may be saved in the day of the Lord Jesus" (ch. 5:4-5).

In such action Paul conceived of his authority as an extension of his spirit to their assemblage, which was his way of understanding his identification with them. When taken with the power of Jesus, which the Corinthians were expected to invoke, it represented that help from beyond which was necessary to overcome the complacency. Paul's first thought, of course, was the expulsion of the man. This he expressed in the technical phraseology of magic,[16] which was in keeping with the rigor of his demand throughout the chapter but which ought not to obscure the fact that the purpose was remedial. For although the curious consignment of the man to Satan for the destruction of his flesh resembles ancient invocations of punishment — in this case probably the rabbinic conception of Satan as capable of carrying out the judgment of God — the important consideration is its ultimate objective " that his [the man's] spirit may be saved in the day of the Lord Jesus."

The modern equivalent of such remedial judgment, and particularly the manner in which the instrumentality of Satan is associated with the possibility of salvation, can only be conjectured. Expressed in the common idiom, it probably concerns the ultimate spiritual benefit accruing to a man who sickens of evil when he has had enough of it. As the evil that befell the prodigal son in the land of his reckless dreams brought him to himself, so it may be that evil, instead of hardening a man's heart, may eventually break it and in this strange manner contribute to his salvation. The parallel in the rehabilitation of certain problematic personalities concerns the desperation seemingly necessary before improvement is possible. Under these circumstances the point of no return seems to be the critical juncture that has to be approached before the inclination or power to act constructively emerges. In the moral and spiritual realm this seems comparable to a strange therapy of law, which, by compelling a man to be consistent in his evil course in what amounts to a form of honesty but is not to be confused with legalism, seems but the negative side of the gospel.

But Paul's primary purpose was to discipline the congregation so that they might discipline the offender. He wanted them to act on their own responsibility and expel him. His main objective was to secure their protection from him, inasmuch as the previous warnings against the destruction of the temple of God and of the body of Christ still pertained. Allowing the man to remain at the risk of such destruction was simply the foolishness of which only pride and arrogance are capable. For the evil of which the man was guilty could not be regarded as of a neutral or static quality but as a corruptive, dynamic influence comparable to the formentative power of yeast in dough. Yeast possessed a religious significance evidently familiar to the Corinthians from a Jewish practice in which yeast (leaven) was a symbol of corruption. Thus Paul can ask, " Do you not know that a little leaven leavens [ferments] the whole lump? " One guilty man is enough to corrupt the whole congregation.

The illustration to which Paul has appealed is the Jews' practice of eliminating from their homes, prior to the Passover, every bit of leavened bread for fear of corruption (ch. 5:7).

Paul's emphasis on the sacrifice of Christ the Paschal Lamb explains such action, which, for its power of appeal, parallels the Jewish Passover as a testimony to divine deliverance. Paul is selecting the crucified Christ — the new Passover — as the means of motivating the Corinthians to clean house and evict the wicked man whose presence is a defiance of the power of Christ to save.

A better analogy, as far as modern man is concerned, although it does not have the religious significance of leavened bread, would be the necessity of sterilization in surgical procedures. The presence of an incestuous man in the congregation is as dangerous as a serious source of infection in a patient's body. The incestuous man, impervious to shame, openly indulging in incest, posed a threat to the congregation comparable to the threat posed by infection, against which modern surgery would take the utmost precaution. When the danger is thus recognized, Paul's desire to protect the congregation not only from the man but from itself will be better appreciated. The insidious nature of sexual license and perversion is not to be lightly considered. For they can work their way into a congregation or a member organization, and by always remaining beneath the surface, corrupt its life. In such instances the temptation toward complacency may be evident in an unwillingness to inform on the guilty parties or to take appropriate disciplinary action. A fear of involvement or of retaliation may discourage it, but such fear is related either to a pride of independence that accepts no responsibility for the actions of others, or to a pride of popularity that desires nothing else but to be well regarded by all.

After discussing the incestuous man, Paul turns to another problem of discipline. It is related to that same condition of spirit and outlook upon life which was responsible for the dissensions, the idolatrous loyalties, and the complacent attitude toward incest. It is another expression of that same pride and arrogance which to this point in the letter have so seriously complicated the life of the church. Christians, in a disgraceful spectacle, had instituted legal action against one another in pagan courts of law. They were probably disposed to litigation by background and temperament, and their action was not exceptional, but in its broader significance was indicative of the common tendency to quarrel over trivialities (ch. 6:2). What is particularly disturbing to Paul is the fact that they had turned to unbelievers to settle their differences. "When one of you has a grievance against a brother, does he dare go to law before the unrighteous instead of the saints? " (ch. 6:1.) Their appeal to pagan courts was a consequence of their inability to arbitrate their own disputes and to exercise that mutuality of discipline expected of a faith whose gospel was a message of reconciliation. It seems that they had attempted arbitration among themselves, but for some reason, probably a whimsical popular opinion, they had turned to those least qualified to judge. As a consequence, Paul's question is almost despairing in its tone: " Can it be that there is no man among you wise enough to decide between members of the brotherhood, but brother goes to law against brother, and that before unbelievers? " (6:5-6). It was more than a matter of Paul's Jewish tradition which was strongly opposed to the thought of suing a fellow member of the faith in a Gentile court, on the ground that such action constituted an effrontery to the sacred law. It was his sensitivity to their lovelessness, as his sorrowful comment suggests: " To have lawsuits at all with one another is defeat for you. Why not rather suffer wrong? Why not rather be defrauded? But you yourselves wrong and defraud, and that even your own brethren " (ch. 6:7).

The significant fact was that the suits of law were only the outward legal expression of an inward hostility. The deep sources of animosity that divided Christian from Christian seemed not to have been touched by the profession of the same faith in Christ. They could wrong and defraud one another as if their faith in him were irrelevant to their conduct. At most they were babes in Christ, full of jealousy and strife (ch. 3:3), whose example only called attention to the great variety of hostility that may menace the church from within the lives of its members. Since much hostility may be beneath the level of consciousness, we have an explanation of the curious facility with which quarrels arise over trivialities. The slightest incident may provoke a scene all out of proportion to what would normally be expected. The interplay of motive and action constituting the domestic politics of the church may suddenly erupt with surprising vigor. Sensitive Christians anxious for recognition will maneuver for position, and by stealthy exploitation of a situation, take advantage of their brethren in conduct which in any church is a potential source of lawsuits. The problem that confronted the apostle in ancient Corinth was not, therefore, exceptional but one that is ever present and in need of discipline.

The probability that the litigants were the same persons as those highly confident of their judgments of the apostles confronts us with a further aspect of the problem. This is the contradiction which obtains between their readiness to judge the apostles and their inability to arbitrate their disputes. Confident of their judgments of men to the point of idolatrous devotion, they fall down badly in the settlement of the most trivial matters. Their dependence on pagan lawyers is really an admission of ineptitude of judgment. Instead of idolatrous loyalties to Paul, Apollos, or Cephas, it is now a question of loyalties to lawyers whose allegiance to other gods inevitably qualified these loyalties. In this respect there is a parallel between the lawsuits and the dissensions (ch. 1:10): they are conflicts in which appeals are made to outsiders to confirm and fulfill the feelings of the contenders. The helplessness of the contenders is a function of their pride. They are not merely consulting outsiders but surrendering to them as sources of validation in a manner inconsistent with personal integrity. Their modern counterparts, who are equally confident of their judgments of other people, are so incapable of coping with the immediate problems of their homes, schools, churches, and communities that they are always appealing to outsiders — lawyers, psychiatrists, columnists, and astrologers — indeed, to anyone who will listen to them.

In each of these instances, rigidity of judgment seems to be responsible for ineptitude of judgment. Oftener a sign of weakness than of strength, rigidity of judgment holds to its position without ability to adjust, until an impasse is reached which in turn reveals its implicit helplessness. Unless an outside arbitrator is found, the impasse remains — not infrequently with tragic results. Indeed, the decision to seek outside help may be a hopeful sign that to some extent mitigates the ineptitude of judgment, depending on the quality of the help received, which in the case of the Corinthians was poor.

The conclusion is that worldly wisdom, represented by rigidity of judgment, is unable to solve its problems because it refuses to be judged by God at its center. Its rigidity is a sign of this refusal, so that, with no other norm but itself, it is helpless before the problems created by it. This suggests that a vain, conceited confidence in one's ability to judge others disqualifies one as a competent arbitrator.

Paul recognized that such rigidity was implicitly an eschatological problem. This was implied in cautioning the Corinthians to judge nothing before the coming of the Lord (ch. 4:5). Their judgments of one another were to be only provisional and therefore characterized by that openness which puts an end to rigidity. In his immediate response to the problem of lawsuits his emphasis is again eschatological, as his question indicates: "Do you not know that the saints will judge the world? And if the world is to be judged by you, are you incompetent to try trivial cases? Do you not know that we are to judge angels?" (ch. 2:3). The fact that Paul's appeal is couched in apocalyptic language and speaks of the Messianic privilege of participating in the divine judgment of the evil powers of the world should not distract us from the practical objective that he had in mind. Implicit in his appeal is the reminder that those who are raised through Christ will reign with him. The resurrection means their participation in the Kingdom of God (chs. 2:15; 15:24-25; Rev. 20:4; cf. Matt. 19:28; Luke 22:30). With such a prospect before them, they should realize that the power of the resurrection is present as well as future, and available now for the purpose of discipline.

They should not be fighting to win lawsuits and to achieve worldly victories at the expense of one another, as if such victories were absolute and the present world were ultimate. They should realize that there is a greater victory, which God has already won in Christ in raising him from the dead, in which they will share, and by virtue of which they will rule the world. The glory they achieve by winning a lawsuit, like the hollow glory of boasting of men, fades into insignificance compared with the glory that shall be revealed to them (Rom. 8:18). The glory of a legal victory is only the glory of talk — the talk by which it was achieved. But "the Kingdom of God does not consist in talk but in power" (I Cor. 4:20). The lawsuits, like all comparable church quarrels, are an indication that the participants have absolutized immediate goals — those defined by themselves. They are a sign that the participants have forgotten the one overall goal that gives ultimate meaning to life and saves them — the resurrection of the dead and the power it will confer upon them. Worldly enslavement to immediacy has blinded them to the joy of living and working in the context of this eschatological motivation.

IX

SPIRITUAL LIBERTINISM
6:12-20

6 *" All things are lawful for me," but not all things are helpful. " All things are lawful for me," but I will not be enslaved by anything.* [13] *" Food is meant for the stomach and the stomach for food " — and God will destroy both one and the other. The body is not meant for immorality, but for the Lord, and the Lord for the body.* [14] *And God raised the Lord and will also raise us up by his power.* [15] *Do you not know that your bodies are members of Christ? Shall I therefore take the members of Christ and make them members of a prostitute? Never!* [16] *Do you not know that he who joins himself to a prostitute becomes one body with her? For, as it is written, " The two shall become one."* [17] *But he who is united to the Lord becomes one spirit with him.* [18] *Shun immorality. Every other sin which a man commits is outside the body; but the immoral man sins against his own body.* [19] *Do you not know that your body is a temple of the Holy Spirit within you, which you have from God? You are not your own;* [20] *you were bought with a price. So glorify God in your body.*

The pastoral problems of the first seven chapters of the letter, which may appear to be somewhat independent of one another, will be recognized on closer examination to be interrelated. The idolatrous loyalties (chs. 1 to 4) and the failure to discipline (chs. 5 to 6:11) have a common origin in worldly wisdom. Together they anticipate the sexual problems of chs. 6 and 7. This is because the eroticism discussed in chs.

6 and 7 is implicit in the jealousy and strife discussed in chs. 1 to 6:11 which is expressive of the pride that characterizes worldly wisdom. To be more specific, the believer who joins himself to a prostitute and becomes one body with her is only exemplifying another form of idolatrous loyalty. The depravity of conscience thus exemplified is related to that of the incestuous man and the complacent congregation to which he belonged.

It will come as a surprise to the conventional Christian accustomed to strictness of sexual morality that Paul should consider the problem of a believer's having relations with a prostitute. Why he should even discuss the matter and thus exhibit a patience that could be mistaken for laxity seems inconsistent in the light of strict morality. The truth, however, is that Paul understood the Corinthian situation better than the conventional Christian realizes. For those to whom he refers had only recently emerged from a religious tradition in which there was a different conception of sexual morality from that of the Hebrew-Christian tradition. Corinth was one of the most immoral cities of the Roman Empire. The sexual license in Greco-Roman city life is well known. But the problem confronting Paul was less likely this wider problem of public morality than the conduct of those who, having turned to the Christian faith, found their old religious habits and attitudes clinging to them.

The practice of prostitution associated with the temples of various deities in the Greco-Oriental world is illustrative of the difference of religious tradition in respect to sexuality. In Corinth the worship of Aphrodite in the temple sacred to her name had had a long reputation of this description. Situated on Acro-Corinthus, the mountain to the southwest, which could be seen from every direction, it had dominated the city. In this as in other religions the practice of prostitution was a solemn act of devotion to the deity acclaimed. The temple prostitute was set apart by religious ceremony, and her office was hallowed by religious authority. She was considered a sacred woman, and union with her was regarded as a sacramental act. The worshiper frequently believed that it procured for him those wider benefits of fecundity evident in abundant harvests and larger flocks and herds. To make light of such worship would be deeply resented.

Gnosticism was another influence that could have turned the recent convert back as easily to public prostitution as to the religious form of it. In its interpretation of the relation between religion and sex, it alternated between libertinism and asceticism, according to its attitude toward the body. In general, contempt for the body led to libertinism, whereas fear of the body led to asceticism. Although in either instance the reasons were complex, contempt for the body consisted in the failure to take it seriously, whereas fear of the body consisted in the desire to avoid contamination.[17] Although it is not known to what extent the problem confronting Paul was a reversion to temple prostitution, the probability is that some variety of gnostic libertinism was influential.

The libertines seem to have made two claims, both of which were more than theoretical, inasmuch as they motivated immoral conduct. The first was that all things are lawful for the believer (ch. 6:12). By such a claim they transformed the freedom they had in Christ into a freedom apart from Christ. In doing this they had probably seized upon an utterance of Paul, lifted it out of context, and given it a meaning opposite to what it originally possessed. As with any evangelical doctrine which, when separated from Christ, is dangerous, his doctrine that the believer is not under law but under grace would be susceptible to perversion. For there always seem to be those who fail to see that freedom from law means freedom for Christ, and never freedom to do as they like in his name (cf. Rom. 6:1, 15).

We do not know precisely what interpretation the libertines gave to the claim that all things are lawful for the believer. Ancient gnosticism was more subtle and complex than its speculative character suggests, particularly in view of certain affinities that it has with modern existentialism and depth psychology.[18] It could have been that they felt so purified through their experience of Christ (gnosis) that not even illicit relations with a prostitute would be considered capable of corrupting their purity. Or, more frankly, they could have been so conceited in sanctity that they held temptation in contempt. Should such extremes seem limited to the ancient libertines, it may be well to recall that a similar supposition sometimes emerges in emotional forms of the Christian faith in any period of history. The participants indulge in a greater degree of sexual freedom among themselves because they feel that unto the pure all things are pure (Titus 1:15).

Or it could have been that the libertines held the moral law in contempt, which was not infrequently the case among the gnostics. This could have meant that they regarded it as only the subjective (conscience) counterpart of the inexorable fate by which an alien world imprisons the allegedly free and divine spirit of man. On this presupposition it would be obligatory to defy the moral law in the interests of freedom, in a manner not unlike those who would now defy the moral law because they regard it as essentially bourgeois. But apart from possible gnostic interpretations of the claim that all things are lawful for the believer, there should not be too much surprise that the Corinthian libertines saw nothing incompatible between faith in Christ and their immoral conduct. For the extent to which faith and doubtful sexual conduct may be found together in the same person in modern times, in what is known as the double life, is by all ordinary standards often incredible.

What the libertines had done with their freedom in Christ was to transform it into a pure, irrational, neutral form of freedom, which without the constraint of love could only mean that Christ was no longer definitive of it. Consequently, it was dangerous. For if all things are lawful in the interest of pure freedom — that is, pure freedom as self-definitive, to which the name of Christ is falsely given — it means not only the end of the law but the end of love. It is a lawless, loveless freedom for which all things are permissible and which is therefore indicative of an abandonment to the irrational, of which prostitution, religious or irreligious, is symbolical. It was this abandonment,

this peculiar form of slavery deceptively implicit in such freedom, that Paul probably had in mind when he retorted that he
would not be enslaved by anything (ch. 6:12). Its resemblance
to modern nihilistic existential freedom, with its social and
political implications, will be evident. Its sexual expression is
therefore not an isolated problem.

The second claim the libertines seem to have made was that
sex is of the same order as physical hunger. To what extent
this claim was a practical inference from the Christian abandonment of Jewish dietary laws, applying the same freedom to
sex as applied to food, is not clear. At least it was a way of ex-
onerating the practice of pure freedom in the realm of the
sexual. Needless to say, Paul was quick to deny the claim and
to assert that the sexual function is not an appetite comparable
to physical hunger. He drew a sharp line between them, permitting neither the Corinthians nor the modern exponent of
sexual freedom to equate them. " ' Food is meant for the stomach and the stomach for food ' — and God will destroy both
one and the other. The body is not meant for immorality, but
for the Lord, and the Lord for the body. And God raised the
Lord and will also raise us up by his power. . . . Every other
sin which a man commits is outside the body; but the immoral
man sins against his own body." (Ch. 6:13-14, 18.)

Paul means that food and the stomach have only a temporal
significance, and they are both subject to death and decay. But
the body has an eschatological significance defined by the resurrection. To understand the distinction it is necessary to recognize that Paul's use of the term " body " is practically
equivalent to the term " person," comparable in meaning to the
suffix " body " in such familiar English words as " anybody "
or " everybody." Consequently, it is the person of the believer,
whose destiny is identifiable with the resurrection, that is
sharply distinguished from the organic, as represented by stomach and food.

Paul's contention is that the sexual function involves the
person (or personality) in a way in which hunger and eating
never do. This is implied in his statement that " every other

sin which a man commits is outside the body; but the immoral man sins against his own body." Sex requires another person in all the complexity of his personality for its satisfaction, whereas hunger requires only food, a physical substance. To conceive of the satisfaction of sex on the same level as hunger is to reduce the other person to the same status as food — that of impersonal substance, merely a physical means. One can eat alone. But God has arranged it that the sexual function requires two persons, male and female, a dichotomy involving the whole human race and within which the ordinance of marriage leads to the establishment of a permanent union that is the foundation of family life. There is no corresponding ordinance for hunger and food. The insight into the personal connotation of sexuality that Paul thus displays is consistent with the recent recognition that sexual problems are less frequently isolated problems of the function itself than symptoms of personality problems. When the immoral man sins against himself by his sexual misdemeanor, he has often already sinned against himself in the context of his deeper personal problem.

The decisive consideration for Paul is the eschatological destiny of the personal. Since sex is intimately bound up with the personal, sex and eschatology are also bound up together. This, in effect, is what the Corinthian libertines and their modern counterparts deny by their equation of sex with hunger, thus making it less personal than physiological. However, the fact that sex is primarily a function for the procreation of new beings and necessarily so because of the dying off of the race, links it inevitably to the eschatological question of the beginning and the end. This inevitable association is unwittingly revealed in the vulgar justification of sexual indulgence by the hedonistic appeal of pleasure now because of death tomorrow. With no hereafter as a positive hope, all things are lawful. Sex becomes an ultimate, if not a substitute, religion. Libido replaces God. Inasmuch as sex, along with the personal, is perishable and ultimately inconsequential, the fatalistic quality of such immorality contrasts sharply with Paul's eschatological hope. For him the resurrection of the body (ch. 6:13-14), already anticipated in his present union with Christ, is the destiny that forbids union with a prostitute and denies the doctrine of the libertines. This is why Paul introduces the resurrection so early in the letter, emphasizing, no doubt, that believers are presently raised with Christ.

Any union with another person that does violence to this present echatological union with Christ, signified by the indwelling of the Holy Spirit and the unique love (agape) correlative with it, is forbidden. It is more than immorality. It is a sin against Christ. Thus Paul declares: " He who is united to the Lord becomes one spirit with him. Shun immorality. . . . Do you not know that your body is a temple of the Holy Spirit within you, which you have from God? You are not your own; you were bought with a price. So glorify God in your body." (Ch. 6:17-20.) Here we have the sharpest contrast between the gnostic and the evangelical conceptions of the body — the one with a low regard for it, the other with a high regard; the one viewing it as a prison house of the human spirit, the other as a temple of the Holy Spirit.

This is the context of Paul's sharp retort: "Do you not know that your bodies are members of Christ? Shall I therefore take the members of Christ and make them members of a prostitute? Never! Do you not know that he who joins himself to a prostitute becomes one body with her? For it is written, ' The two shall become one ' " (ch. 6:15-16). The question is how such an illicit union does violence to the believer's union with Christ. What precisely was wrong with the conduct of the libertines? To recapitulate — we have seen that it was an expression of a pure, irrational freedom that was essentially lawless and loveless. We have also seen that it depersonalized the sexual function to a physiological level, probably as a consequence of a world view that accorded man no significant destiny. The important point is that these two observations have one thing in common. The illicit sexual relation is indicative of an absence of love as an eschatological category — that love represented by the term " agape." Thus it is essentially a form of godlessness of the same character as the Johannine text describes: " He who does not love does not know God; for God is love " (I John 4:8). This prompts a further observation that immorality and implicit atheism are curiously correlative.

But the godlessness of the illicit sexual union does violence to the humanity of the participants. A man who unites with a prostitute indulges in an act that is mutually self-destructive. It is destructive of her humanity under the form of femininity and of his under the form of masculinity. To understand how this happens we have to understand the Biblical significance of the text Paul quotes: " The two shall become one " (ch. 6:16). In Genesis the statement is a conclusion from the creation of woman out of man and indicates their primal unity (Gen. 2:18-24). A man leaves his father and mother and cleaves to his wife, and is of one flesh with her, because of this original unity. Such action, which is integral to the created order, is prior to the fall of man and is therefore under the connotation of innocence. The text that follows makes this clear: " And the man and his wife were both naked, and were not ashamed " (Gen. 2:25).

With the entrance of sin, however, innocence was distorted into a form of love characterized by desire, by self-seeking, and by man's losing himself in himself as if he were a god, which was ultimately a denial of his humanity[19] (cf. Gen. 3:5). It was no more possible for the two to become one, as originally designed by the gracious, creative act of God. Instead, they had brought upon themselves the sad plight depicted in Gen. 3:16: " To the woman he said, ' I will greatly multiply your pain in childbearing; in pain you shall bring forth children, yet your desire shall be for your husband, and he shall rule over you.' " This meant that the man-woman relationship was blighted with the possibility of enmity between them — the man tempted to lord it over the woman and the woman tempted to be resentful of him and of her femininity. There could be no real union now except by overcoming the enmity and the sin implicit in it. But the sexual act was incapable of this. It could not overcome the enmity and the sin. Consequently, it is doubtful to what extent it ever achieves what some denote as an ontological unity (henosis) between the man and the woman.[20] Instead, all that it seems to achieve is a formal union in which children are conceived in sin (Ps. 51:5). This, of course, has the characteristic " oneness " that belongs to the particularity of the personal. In this respect it could be described as the unity involved in " falling in love," in which the personal is respected, but which is not equivalent to the unity represented by the evangelical understanding of reconciliation. Such love could be classified only as a higher form of eros.

Thus, for a man to join himself to a prostitute would involve a formal union with her, but without a falling in love it would be subpersonal. Yet it would retain a personal connotation with respect to the intimacy it involved. There would inhere in the relationship a tendency toward the " oneness " characteristic of the more personal type of union. The memory of episode, the emotional conditioning, and the mixture of motives would leave their mark on the psyche. To this extent he would be one with her. But without love and responsibility the union would not only fall short of the unity that comes of a personal relationship but would be destructive of the spiritual unity that comes of reconciliation through Christ. For a Christian to enter such a union would be a denial of his faith and of the reality of the living relationship that binds him to his Lord. For how could he be involved in an episode that would leave such a mark upon his psyche, that would bind him to a prostitute at this subpersonal level? How could he exhibit so little responsibility for her and thus be unreconciled to her through the Lord he professed to love? Or how could he indulge in a denial of their mutual humanity, which is expressed in their masculinity and femininity as signs of the grace of God in the act of creation? For such a denial would be a denial of the connotation of innocence representative of the claim that God still had upon them despite their guilt.

As a corollary of these observations, it is helpful to realize that the sexual life is never so truly expressed and fulfilled and beautified as when Christ is permitted to claim and redeem it. By his power it is so taken up into the personality and incorporated into his redemptive purpose as to become a great blessing. The immoral person, contrary to his perverted conception of his body, is really the one who fails to experience the true joy of sexual life. His eroticism is a sign of his failure to love and therefore of his implicit atheism, both of which are expressive of the false wisdom of the world. Thus we can understand why the Ephesian letter emphasizes that Christ and his church, as the bridegroom and the bride, constitute the union that is normative to marriage. This unity is definitive, in its reconciled form, of the two who become one according to the Genesis passage (Eph. 5:21-33).

X

MARITAL ASCETICISM

7:1-15, 20-24, 32-38

7 *Now concerning the matters about which you wrote. It is well for a man not to touch a woman.*[2] *But because of the temptation to immorality, each man should have his own wife and each woman her own husband.* [3] *The husband should give to his wife her conjugal rights, and likewise the wife to her husband.* [4] *For the wife does not rule over her own body, but the husband does; likewise the husband does not rule over his own body, but the wife does.* [5] *Do not refuse one another except perhaps by agreement for a season, that you may devote yourselves to prayer; but then come together again, lest Satan tempt you through lack of self-control.* [6] *I say this by way of concession, not of command.* [7] *I wish that all were as I myself am. But each has his own special gift from God, one of one kind and one of another.*

8 *To the unmarried and the widows I say that it is well for them to remain single as I do.* [9] *But if they cannot exercise self-control, they should marry. For it is better to marry than to be aflame with passion.*

10 *To the married I give charge, not I but the Lord, that the wife should not separate from her husband* [11] *(but if she does, let her remain single or else be reconciled to her husband) — and that the husband should not divorce his wife.*

12 *To the rest I say, not the Lord, that if any brother has a wife who is an unbeliever, and she consents to live with him, he should not divorce her.* [13] *If any woman has a husband who is an unbeliever, and he consents to live with her, she should not divorce him.* [14] *For the unbelieving husband is consecrated through his wife, and the unbelieving wife is consecrated through her hus-*

94

band. *Otherwise, your children would be unclean, but as it is they are holy.* [15] *But if the unbelieving partner desires to separate, let it be so; in such a case the brother or sister is not bound. For God has called us to peace.*

[20] *Every one should remain in the state in which he was called.* [21] *Were you a slave when called? Never mind. But if you can gain your freedom, avail yourself of the opportunity.* [22] *For he who was called in the Lord as a slave is a freedman of the Lord. Likewise he who was free when called is a slave of Christ.* [23] *You were bought wtih a price; do not become slaves of men.* [24] *So, brethren, in whatever state each was called, there let him remain with God.*

[32] *I want you to be free from anxieties. The unmarried man is anxious about the affairs of the Lord, how to please the Lord;* [33] *but the married man is anxious about worldly affairs, how to please his wife,* [34] *and his interests are divided. And the unmarried woman or girl is anxious about the affairs of the Lord, how to be consecrated in body and spirit; but the married woman is anxious about worldly affairs, how to please her husband.* [35] *I say this for your own benefit, not to lay any restraint upon you, but to promote good order and to secure your undivided devotion to the Lord.*

[36] *If any one thinks that he is not behaving properly toward his betrothed, if his passions are strong, and it has to be, let him do as he wishes: let them marry — it is no sin.* [37] *But whoever is firmly established in his heart, being under no necessity but having his desire under control, and has determined this in his heart, to keep her as his betrothed, he will do well.* [38] *So that he who marries his betrothed does well; and he who refrains from marriage will do better.*

———

The sexual problem that confronted Paul in the seventh chapter was the opposite of the one that confronted him in the sixth chapter. Now it was asceticism instead of libertinism, a rejection of sexuality instead of an irresponsible abandonment to it — a reaction against it as rigid and as uncompromising as the previous attraction to it had been promiscuous. In a word, the problem was that those involved seemed to have equated all sexuality with sin including normal marital relations. Consequently they regarded matrimony as sinful rather than holy and either discouraged couples from marrying or convinced those already married to separate.

The source of the problem seems to have been the same gnostic tendencies as before, but they were now productive of a fear of sex rather than an abandonment to it. The influences were undoubtedly complex and the gnosticism not clearly defined, so that we have to allow for other possible factors contributing to the asceticism — for instance, the natural reaction of any society to the excesses of libertinism, and not improbably, an ascetic strain from Judaistic sources.[21] Beyond these, of course, was the extent to which asceticism was gradually inundating the Mediterranean world. In this respect it "was as universal and as indifferent to race and creed and nationality as were the syncretistic and individualistic tendencies. It pervaded philosophy and religion. Like a mighty tide it swept onward, from the first century B.C., from the east over the west, gathering momentum as it forced its way into every serious view of life."[22]

It is important to recognize that the fear of sex, now in the form of a religious revulsion against it, was as much a product of worldly wisdom as the libertinism it condemned. The gnostic conception of the divine spark or spirit imprisoned in man is not in principle different from the essential meaning of eros. The repudiation of sex should not be permitted to obscure the fact that eros may be expressed in a higher attenuated form. A chastity maintained only by its negation of sex is as sexocentric in its conception of purity as libertinism is in its conception of pleasure. Such chastity, in its appeal to the popular mind, may represent a form of worldly wisdom that is part of the discipline required for social and economic security against the insecurity libertinism inevitably causes. It is eros disciplining itself without any essential change of nature. This is suggested by those social systems, of which communism is an example, in which an emphasis on chastity may emerge without any significant religious motivation. The worldly reasons why

the Corinthian puritans of ch. 7 might appeal to many over the
libertines of ch. 6 should expose the fact that the former had
not really advanced in authentic Christian faith over the latter.
These reasons would be similar to those which explain why the
elder brother in the parable is often more popular than the
prodigal, and the Pharisee more popular than the publican. For
in the last analysis, if atheism and immorality are strangely correlative, there are circumstances in which atheism and asceticism are strangely correlative, and this correlation is more
dangerous both in its dynamic and in the subtlety of its appeal.

The effect of asceticism upon the Corinthian church was
that some persons had begun to abstain from the sexual relations normal to marriage, presumably because they felt that
these were sinful and that matrimony compromised the purity
of their spiritual life. This was why Paul had to declare that a
husband should give his wife her conjugal rights and similarly
the wife her husband (ch. 7:3), and that the wife should not
separate from her husband nor the husband divorce his wife
(ch. 7:10-11). The ascetic emphasis on purity was creating
serious problems of marital disharmony. In some instances it
was preventing those from marrying whose moral life would
be better served by marriage (ch. 7:8-9). In other instances it
was particularly responsible for disrupting marriages in which
husband or wife had become a believer without the conversion
of the other. The impression had arisen that if the marital union
of believers were sinful, a similar union of believer with unbeliever would be doubly sinful. Although Paul had no word of
the Lord to cover the situation, he advocated charity, indicating that if the unbelieving spouse consents, the marriage should
not be broken; if not, he should be allowed to go (ch. 7:12-
15). Charity especially pertains to the benefit which the maintenance of such a marriage would have for the children involved (ch. 7:14).

The same asceticism was responsible for the promotion of
spiritual betrothals, the nature of which is obscure (ch. 7:36-
38). These may have involved engaged couples bound by af-
fection and faith who had resolved to preserve the relationship

instead of proceeding to matrimony. Or they may have been a form of spiritual marriage — a union of two on earth in anticipation of heaven but without sexual consummation. Traces of this phenomenon appear in the second century from Antioch to Rome, Syria to North Africa, and in Egypt. Early in the fourth century certain synods of the church denounced the practice for the scandals that Paul feared.

As thus outlined, the effect of asceticism on marriage was indicative of an emphasis on celibacy and virginity motivated by a loveless zeal for purity. Implicit in it was probably a gnostic conception of the ascent of the spirit to the Most High God, which at the same time was conceived as an escape from the body. Definitive of the relation between the believer and Christ, from this point of view it would be representative of another idolatrous loyalty — this time to Christ as the prototype of such purity. This is not to claim that the idolatrous loyalty would be identical with that of the Christ-party of ch. 1, but the possibility should not be dismissed. It is rather the claim that the loyalty to such a christ was productive of a party of celibates and virgins that divided the body of Christ and contributed to dissention in the church. The unhappy circumstances of marital disharmony, separation, and divorce was sufficient proof of it. The christ who was thus portrayed came between husbands and wives and broke up their marriages, and between those who contemplated marriage, and broke up their engagements. Loyalty to him in no way exemplified the gospel injunction of greater love to him than to father, mother, husband, or wife, because he was not the same Christ as proclaimed in the gospel. He was the christ of ascetic chastity, who could scarcely have been a man, born of a woman, unless he and the woman by definition were devoid of sexuality.

In the subsequent history of the church the parallels that obtained between the Corinthian ascetics and the catholic fathers are not without significance despite the fact that the latter generally repudiated gnosticism. For the attempt to derive the asceticism of the fathers from a certain partiality of Paul toward celibacy and virginity is a far cry from his permissive and charitable attitude to marriage. The extremity of their views finds no precedent in him. Nowhere do we find in Paul a comparable attitude to that of Tertullian, for instance, who spoke of marriage as a " voluptuous disgrace, frivolous and impure." Nor do we find a resemblance to Jerome, who could praise marriage only because it gave the church more virgins. Nor can we imagine Paul, like Origen, emasculating himself in literal obedience to Matt. 19:12.[23]

On the contrary the conduct of the early catholic fathers and saints reminds us more of the Corinthian ascetics than of Paul. For it has been observed of the asceticism so prevalent in the patristic period that " whenever any strong religious impulse fell upon a husband or wife its first effect was to make a happy union impossible. The immense place this order of ideas occupies in the hortatory writings of the fathers and of the legends of the saints must be familiar to all who have any knowledge of this department of literature. Thus to give but a few examples — St. Nilus when he already had two children was seized with a longing for the prevailing asceticism and his wife was persuaded after many tears to consent to their separation. St. Ammon in the night of his marriage proceeded to greet his bride with a harangue upon the evils of the married state and they agreed in consequence to separate." [24]

However, the extent to which Paul himself contributed to the asceticism of the patristic period cannot be ignored, since he is often cited in support of celibacy and virginity. It is evident, of course, that he opposed the asceticism of the Corinthians in the particular form in which it appeared — probably a gnostic form. But in his opposition he revealed a certain asceticism of his own which in subsequent ecclesiastical practice has often been misunderstood.

Paul's asceticism may be detected in his observation that it is well for a man not to touch a woman, but because of the temptation to immorality each man should have his own wife and each woman her own husband (I Cor. 7:1-2). The negative function which he here attributes to marriage reappears almost immediately in the fifth verse in his sensitivity to married couples' being tempted of Satan through lack of self-control. It appears more explicitly in his advice to the unmarried and widows to marry rather than be aflame with passion (ch. 7:9) and finally, at the end of the chapter, in his approval of the self-restraint of the betrothed who resolve to forgo marriage (ch. 7:37). In each instance his concern for self-control suggests that sexuality involves a Freudianlike dynamic that should never be lightly considered. Marriage fulfills a negative function in its exercise of restraint — in keeping sexuality within its proper bounds. As far as such a conception goes, it could be regarded as an inferior view of marriage. But the extent to which it represented asceticism on the one hand or practical realism on the other, valid for both modern and ancient life, is a question that must not be evaded. Insofar as it represented the latter, Paul's negative conception of the function of marriage resembles his negative conception of the function of the law, which is enunciated in the letter to the Galatians (Gal. 3:23 to 4:2). For marriage, like the law, is a jailer holding sexuality in protective custody, or a custodian keeping it under discipline.

There is a less ambiguous asceticism, however, in Paul's approval of the suspension of conjugal rights for the sake of a season of prayer (I Cor. 7:5). For although he advocated, over against the Corinthian ascetics, that husbands and wives not refuse one another their conjugal rights, the fact that he makes this exception for prayer indicates that in his mind there was a certain incompatibility between sexuality and spirituality even in marriage. This is evidently one of the reasons for his choice of celibacy, and a clarification of what he meant in the opening verse, where he says that it is well for a man — presumably a spiritual man — not to touch a woman. It is also the motive that inspired his approval of the betrothed who resolved to refrain from marriage. His comment that the latter do better than those who marry (v. 38) has reference again to spirituality.

Another factor that entered into Paul's asceticism and his choice of celibacy was the anxiety he associated with matrimony and the resultant division of the believer's loyalty to Christ. " The married man is anxious about worldly affairs, how to please his wife, and his interests are divided. . . . The married woman is anxious about worldly affairs, how to please her husband." (Ch. 7:33-34.) There is an anxiety accompanying marriage, according to Paul, that is presumably associated with its negative function as a means of controlling sexuality. For if, as we have observed, he recognized in sexuality a Freudianlike dynamic requiring strict control, such anxiety could well be the inevitable tension implicit in such control. Husbands who are always concerned how they may please their wives and wives how they may please their husbands are not the happiest persons — which raises the question of how many happy marriages Paul had seen.

Such a one-sided skepticism toward marriage, whatever its origin — sexually or socially, having regard both to Paul's upbringing and to the state of ancient society generally — was, to say the least, uncomplimentary to those of his fellow apostles and laborers in the gospel who were married. There were Priscilla and Aquila, for example, the hospitality of whose home Paul enjoyed while he was in Corinth (Acts 18:1-3), whom he describes in Romans as his fellow workers in Christ Jesus, who risked their necks for his life, and to whom not only he but also all the churches of the Gentiles gave thanks (Rom. 16:3-4). It was they who, according to The Acts, took no less than Apollos aside and " expounded to him the way of God more accurately " (Acts 18:26). Nor can we believe that Paul was complimentary to Peter and those other apostles and brothers of the Lord whom he recognizes later in the letter as availing themselves of the right to be accompanied by their wives (I Cor. 9:5). Roman Catholic exegetes who on the basis of the Vulgate maintain that this refers to unmarried women are equally uncomplimentary. The doubtful propriety of the apostles' being accompanied by unmarried women on their missionary journeys is not a commendable alternative.

But whatever may be said of the one-sidedness of Paul's conception of marriage, it is clear that his attitude was permissive.

For although he exhibits a certain partiality toward the Corinthian ascetics, he does not impose his view upon the church. Even when he expresses the wish that all were as he (ch. 7:7), he immediately comments that each has his own special gift from God, one of one kind and one of another. And even when he expresses at greater length his preference for celibacy and virginity on the ground that they allow freedom from the anxiety which to him is characteristic of matrimony, he is careful to qualify his statement in a similar manner. He has no desire to lay any restraint upon them (ch. 7:35). But still more indicative of his permissive attitude is the manner in which he distinguishes what is only his opinion from what is the word or command of the Lord (vs. 6, 12, 25, 40). In three out of four instances in which he makes this distinction it is clear that his preference for the unmarried state is only a matter of opinion. It is not a requirement to be imposed upon the church or upon his fellow apostles or workers in the gospel. Celibacy and virginity are not obligatory upon the ministry. Consequently we see that in spite of his asceticism and of his partiality toward the Corinthian ascetics he never compromises the freedom he and others have in Christ.

The importance of this observation in relation to the third and final factor determining Paul's asceticism, namely, its eschatological perspective, should not be overlooked. The whole of the seventh chapter is charged with a high degree of eschatological expectation, which conditions everything Paul has to say. He is conscious at every point that the appointed time is short and that the form of the world is passing away (vs. 29-31). It affected not only his conception of marriage but his conception of social and economic life, as we see from his plea that every believer remain in the same state in which he was called — circumcised and uncircumcised, slave and freedman (vs. 18-22). In a word, sexuality and marriage, as other forms of human behavior Paul mentions — sorrowing and rejoicing, buying and selling (v. 30) — are only of relative importance when confronted with the End of the World — the Day of Resurrection. But this does not condemn them as evil. They are temporary, but not of themselves opposed to God. Consequently there is an asceticism that is only another name for the recognition of the relativity and temporality of sexuality and marriage and all other forms of human behavior. But it differs from the asceticism of Paul's Corinthian opponents in that, unlike theirs, it is not a law — not something fixed and obligatory and normative for all. It is an asceticism that is free in relation to the End of the World as Paul conceived it. Indeed, if we wish to see how absurd it is to transform his asceticism into a law valid for all time without regard to the urgency of his eschatological expectations, we need only take what he says of every believer's remaining in the same state in which he was called, and transform this into a law valid for all time. It would then be definitive of the most rigid caste system or social and political *status quo* imaginable. The freedom derivative of its eschatological context would have been completely dissipated. All that is known as agape would have departed from it.

The modern parallel to the asceticism of ancient Corinth which will probably come to mind will be the equation of sexuality with sin in marital life. Although the extremes of ancient Corinth will be largely avoided, the same presuppositions will be recognized in a negative type of morality that emphasizes chastity at the expense of a wholesome attitude to sexuality. As a type of morality frequently inculcated by parents into their children, it tends to interfere with the marital life of the latter when they mature and establish homes and families of their own. Its association of sexuality with the unseemly and shameful creates a guilt complex that is not resolved even within the context of marriage. The larger perspective within which it acquires significance is one that regards spirit as superior to matter, and reason as superior to desire, in a gradation which in every case relegates the sexual to an inferior level, as though sexual sin were by definition worse than spiritual or rational sin. But such morality, typical of Roman Catholic rigorism and of Protestant puritanism, and of a piety beyond both traditions and even outside the church in a conventional form of respectability, is not the most significant modern parallel to the asceticism of ancient Corinth. Because it is more conspicuous as well as more susceptible to criticism from the standpoint of a wholesome acceptance of the body as created by God, we should not assume that it is the parallel upon which our attention should be mainly directed. For there is another, more subtle form of modern asceticism, whose negation of sexuality is characterized by its indirectness.

This asceticism is a negation not of sexuality as such but of masculinity and femininity. It therefore involves a distortion of what may be generally designated as man-woman relationships in modern society, and consequently these relationships within the church and as they pertain to the institution of marriage. It is an asceticism characterized by an attitude toward life, and by a pattern of behavior, indicative of a personality that tends to negate the particular gender with which God has endowed a person. In women it is characterized by revolt against the fact that they are women, which is at the same time a secret wish that they were men. It is revealed by a tendency to act like men and to pride themselves on doing what men do as well as men. For this reason they tend to exemplify an emotionally competitive attitude toward men which in marriage as well as in the work of the church tends to foster an unfortunate kind of rivalry.

In men it is a rejection of masculinity in the sense of substituting a submissiveness tantamount to a false form of femininity. It is revealed in a tendency to refrain from the acceptance of those responsibilities which women have a right to expect of them as men, particularly of those which their wives and children have a right to expect. The consequences of such ineptness, which is indicative of a failure to sever the apron strings of an inordinate attachment to their mothers, are frequently disastrous both in marriage and in the work of the church. In this regard the comment of a distinguished psychiatric authority is most revealing: " The chief sin of men with respect to their wives and families," he says, " is not harshness, nor parsimony, nor tyranny, nor injustice, nor eccentricity, but passivity." Under passivity he includes overdependence, inattentiveness, helplessness, overmeekness, indifference, neglect, and (in extreme cases) desertion.[25]

Corresponding to the pseudo masculinity of women and the pseudo femininity of men, in what may be properly regarded as neoasceticism, is a pseudo goodness symbolical of their goal of achievement. In the simpler asceticism, with its direct negation of sexuality, goodness was identified with chastity and the pattern of life it represented. But in the case of neoasceticism, it is not chastity as such, but the social and economic demands of modern society necessary for secular success that define the pseudo goodness. Women are compelled by these demands, especially as they participate in the same occupational world as men, to act more like men for the sake of success. Men are compelled — and this in relation to their wives and families — to be passive at home because they are preoccupied with their success in the outside world. Their lives are so absorbed by their business and professional interests that they have little time left for their wives and children at home. And their desire to be successful is not unrelated to the deep desire to please others and to be accepted which their mothers have instilled into them as pseudo goodness. In other words, to summarize the comparison with the simpler, older form of asceticism, with its negation of sexuality in the interests of chastity, this neoasceticism involves a negation of femininity and masculinity in the interests of success. The effects upon marital life and upon the attitudes of the unmarried toward such life are no less disastrous than the effects discernible in the Corinthian situation that confronted Paul.

XI

IRRESPONSIBLE FREEDOM

8:1-13; 10:1-12

8 *Now concerning food offered to idols: we know that " all of us possess knowledge." " Knowledge " puffs up, but love builds up. ² If any one imagines that he knows something, he does not yet know as he ought to know. ³ But if one loves God, one is known by him.*

4 Hence, as to the eating of food offered to idols, we know that " an idol has no real existence," and that " there is no God but one." ⁵ For although there may be so-called gods in heaven or on earth — as indeed there are many " gods " and many " lords " — ⁶ yet for us there is one God, the Father, from whom are all things and for whom we exist, and one Lord, Jesus Christ, through whom are all things and through whom we exist.

7 However, not all possess this knowledge. But some, through being hitherto accustomed to idols, eat food as really offered to an idol; and their conscience, being weak, is defiled. ⁸ Food will not commend us to God. We are no worse off if we do not eat, and no better off if we do. ⁹ Only take care lest this liberty of yours somehow become a stumbling block to the weak. ¹⁰ For if any one sees you, a man of knowledge, at table in an idol's temple, might he not be encouraged, if his conscience is weak, to eat food offered to idols? ¹¹ And so by your knowledge this weak man is destroyed, the brother for whom Christ died. ¹² Thus, sinning against your brethren and wounding their conscience when it is weak, you sin against Christ. ¹³ Therefore, if food is a cause of my brother's falling, I will never eat meat, lest I cause my brother to fall.

10 *I want you to know, brethren, that our fathers were all under the cloud, and all passed through the sea, ² and all were baptized into Moses in the cloud and in the sea, ³ and all ate the same supernatural food ⁴ and all drank the same supernatural drink. For they drank from the supernatural Rock which followed them, and the Rock was Christ. ⁵ Nevertheless with most of them God was not pleased; for they were overthrown in the wilderness.*

6 Now these things are warnings for us, not to desire evil as they did. ⁷ Do not be idolaters as some of them were; as it is written, "The people sat down to eat and drink and rose up to dance." ⁸ We must not indulge in immorality as some of them did, and twenty-three thousand fell in a single day. ⁹ We must not put the Lord to the test, as some of them did and were destroyed by serpents; ¹⁰ nor grumble, as some of them did and were destroyed by the Destroyer. ¹¹ Now these things happened to them as a warning, but they were written down for our instruction, upon whom the end of the ages has come. ¹² Therefore let anyone who thinks that he stands take heed lest he fall.

It was the custom in Corinth as elsewhere in the Greco-Roman world to consecrate to a pagan god animals slaughtered for food. The animals were slaughtered not only for religious purposes but for public consumption, and sold on the common market. "For pagans as well as Jews slaughtered ritually and dealt with all slaughtered animals as if they were sacrificial." [26] As a consequence, the meat was a cultic symbol representative of idolatry — not the idolatry of loyalties to religious leaders, as in the earlier chapters, but formal idolatry, explicitly pagan. For the sensitive Christian, this situation created a serious dilemma. As one who probably shared the Jewish aversion to food that was ceremonially unclean, he would be fearful even of the accidental consumption of sacrificial meat and was perhaps confronted with the only alternative — becoming a vegetarian (Rom. 14:2). An additional complication arose from the fact that this formal idolatry was associated with immorality, particularly in the intemperate atmosphere of the temple feasts.

What aggravated the problem was the way in which it affected social relationships, isolating Christians from their pagan friends and relatives and interfering with their participation in public functions. A descriptive reconstruction of the probable circumstances will serve to make this clear:

" When the hunting club of the Artemesians held a banquet, for example, they began by sacrificing part of the meat to Artemis, their patron deity. Or a private party might be given nominally as a ' table of Lord Serapis,' the proceedings being opened by a similar sacrifice. . . . A pagan might invite his friends to dinner. It might be held in some temple; in which case the meat of the slain animal, i.e., a small piece of it, often some uneatable portion like the hair, was first consecrated to the god who was formally supposed to preside at the banquet, which was called a table of Serapis, Isis, or Aesculapius as the case may be. . . . Should the dinner be given at home the host would have the carcass brought back from the temple or he might purchase similar food in the butcher's shop which commonly adjoined the temple." [27]

Under these circumstances a Christian might feel he was insulting his friends either by his failure to attend or by his refusal to eat. If he was deeply sensitive, he might separate from them entirely for fear of the risk. On the other hand, if he ate, he might feel he was compromising his faith in Christ and be burdened with a guilty conscience. If he were weak in the faith, this might prove too much for him and lead to his fall.

What disturbed Paul was the extremely liberal attitude of those who thought there was no harm in eating meat consecrated to idols even to the point of participating in pagan temple feasts (I Cor. 8:10). In the assertion of their freedom they callously disregarded its influence upon the weaker Christian who might have been moved to imitate them. They acknowledged no responsibility for his spiritual destiny. Yet they belonged to the same congregation and professed the same faith. In the proud confidence that nothing in pagan idolatry could harm or undermine their faith, they were unconcerned even though their example contributed to the danger of the spiritual downfall of a fellow Christian. Indeed, their relation to pagan idolatry was not unlike that of the self-confident modern Christian who in the assertion of his freedom largely identifies himself with secularism in his mode of living, choice of friends, and loyalties. His secularism contributes to the defection of weaker Christians, possibly younger members of his church or family. Since individuals vary in their vulnerability to ideological infiltration, it not infrequently happens that an irresponsible broad-mindedness can tempt a weaker Christian into atheism.

The problem pertained to the freedom permitted a Christian along the delicate boundary line dividing faith from idolatry. It became acute at the point of cultic expression, which in this case involved consecrated meat. But it could have been some other symbol had the competitive point of difference between the idolatry and the Christian faith derived from other religious customs or from the secular practices of a modern ideology. For this reason it was less a problem of isolated practices about which Christians may differ as a matter of conscience than a problem possessed of idolatrous or ideological significance. With this qualification it could be said that the meat was incidental to the main problem — the nature and limits of Christian freedom in relation to idolatry. The recognition of this will prevent the easy conclusion that the issue pertains only to the meat and at the present time only to those areas in the world, mainly Asiatic, where Christians are actually confronted with decisions respecting food offered to idols. For there are other situations in the modern world that involve the Christian in a dilemma concerning the extent of his fraternization with those whose religious or ideological perspective involves the rejection of Christ. In such instances, what frequently makes the problem acute is the extent to which his more independent, self-confident fellow Christians participate in organizations and projects whose principles are foreign to the Christian faith and destructive of it.

As a citizen of a totalitarian state, for example, he may see fellow Christians attending organizations whose ideological demands seem to him incompatible with faith. If he fails to attend, severe penalties may be imposed — perhaps the restriction of educational opportunity or of promotion in shop or factory, or the stigma of reactionary tendencies. On the other hand, if he attends, he may feel he is compromising his faith and acting a lie and therefore destroying his integrity. The pangs of guilt may be harder to bear than the persecution that would otherwise be inflicted upon him. If, moreover, he is a man weak in the faith, he may abandon it entirely and in his acceptance of the ideology turn against his fellow Christians with a severity characteristic of such defection.

Or it may be a situation in a part of the world more tolerant of religion, where the Christian finds himself involved in a community service of worship. By the nature of the service the name of Christ is conveniently omitted. Not even an allusion to him is made in the prayers or message in which the focus of attention is on those sentiments acceptable to the widest constituency. The name of God is invoked but without identification or significant content. He is but an anonymous god intended only as a symbol comprehensive of united action. Again the sensitive Christian is in a dilemma. He sees his more liberal-minded brethren participating without any scruples of conscience. He would like to follow their example because he knows that failure to participate may expose him to the accusation of bigotry. But if he participates he may feel he is compromising his faith and virtually denying the One in whom he professes to believe. If he abandons all his sensitivity and cooperates to the fullest extent, he may eventually conclude that it matters little what a man believes. In this state of mind he may be persuaded that faith in a vague, anonymous god has greater claim to validity than faith in Christ.

Or the situation may be less specific than either of these examples. The Christian may find himself identified with an organization in which, because of the secular atmosphere, the mention of anything specifically related to faith is felt by his associates to be foreign. They merely listen with an indifference that is but an empty form of tolerance. They do not know enough either to deny or to affirm what he has said. He is tempted by a comfortable security of silence — to retreat into himself or into a small religious group where he feels at home. Yet the silence leaves him uneasy because he feels that he has compromised his faith and failed to witness. Although there is no particular symbolism, no definite occasion on which the issue comes to a head, the silence is the equivalent of meat offered to an idol. His associates prefer it in the interests of their secularism. But it wounds his conscience, and in the slow process of time destroys his faith.

In these various examples from the modern scene, Paul would probably have been on the side of the more liberal-minded Christians in principle but against their loveless, irresponsible freedom in practice. As in Corinth he would have been disturbed by their lack of evangelical concern for their fellow Christians, particularly those who are weak in the faith. In this he would have detected a failure to appreciate the urgency of eternal salvation as the greatest blessing that can come to any man — a failure that could therefore be regarded as a sin against Christ (ch. 8:12). This is why his warning is so clearly directed against the liberal-minded. Their freedom is destructive of the fellowship definitive of the church as the body of Christ. It is a freedom consistent with the spirit of those who earlier in the letter showed no concern for the fact that their idolatrous loyalties were creating dissensions in the church. This is not to suggest that Paul expected the more liberal-minded to accommodate to any tendency on the part of the weaker Christian to impose his will upon them. Such a possibility would be characteristic of the babe in Christ rather than of the weaker Christian, according to Paul's understanding of the latter.

What seems to have been mainly responsible for this loveless, irresponsible freedom which was causing the trouble in the Corinthian church were certain gnostic tendencies. Although their precise nature is obscure, it is evident that they encouraged the extremely liberal attitude toward the eating of meat consecrated to idols. This is indicated by the fact that Paul connects such liberty with a knowledge that, instead of building up believers in the faith, puffed them up with pride (ch. 8:1). Studies of gnosticism would suggest that such knowledge likely refers more to a form of religious experience than to an intellectual content.[28] Those who had had such experience had presumably seen through idolatry and had emphasized the claim Paul acknowledges, that "'an idol has no real existence'" (ch. 8:4). This was evidently the basis of the freedom they exhibited. Since an idol has no existence, they were convinced it was incapable of defiling meat consecrated to it. Consequently, there was no harm in eating it. As those who possessed such knowledge, they were proud of their freedom — indeed, as Paul says, puffed up about it so that they were more concerned to display it than to assume responsibility for its adverse influence upon their weaker brethren.

As indicated in ch. 10:1-12, their conception of freedom was complicated by a sacramentalism they probably considered supplementary to their religious experience (knowledge). Since the latter was frequently conceived as a potency (*dynamis*), a similar conception of the sacraments would explain the association of the one with the other. In this case the sacraments would provide an added protection that would encourage the liberal-minded to display their freedom with even less fear than before. In what therefore probably amounted to a magical conception, the sacraments would merely heighten the pride they already had in their religious experience. They would feel more secure in the exercise of their freedom.

It was such pride against which Paul seems to have warned in ch. 10:12: "Therefore let any one who thinks that he stands take heed lest he fall." The warning comes as a conclusion to a series of illustrations from the exodus, in which the action of God in delivering and preserving his people is regarded as sacramental. The reference to the sacramental is explicit: "All were baptized into Moses in the cloud and in the sea, and all ate the same supernatural food and all drank the same supernatural drink" (ch. 10:4). But this did not protect them from idolatry and the immorality associated with it. It did not safeguard them in such a manner that they could indulge in an irresponsible freedom within the security it provided. It was not a protection upon which they could presume or which, in magical fashion, operated independently of their action. In selecting these illustrations there is no doubt that Paul had in mind the immediate temptation confronting the Corinthians in eating meat consecrated to idols. The idol feasts — the intemperance and the abandonment which were evidently associated with them — reminded him of the cult of the golden calf in Exodus, the consequences of which were so disastrous for the people of Israel. Hence the specific character of his warning: " Do not be idolaters as some of them were; as it is written, ' The people sat down to eat and drink and rose up to dance.' We must not indulge in immorality as some of them did, . . . and were destroyed by the Destroyer " (10:7-8, 10).

However experiential and sacramental the power by which the Corinthians thought they were free from idolatry and its associated sin, they were dangerously vulnerable to it apart from the question of the weaker Christians. If the latter were vulnerable, so were the former, except in a subtler and less conspicuous manner. The ability to see through idolatry and to recognize that an idol is nothing was not enough to liberate them from the mystery of evil which these represented. Even if such insight were the rationale of a religious experience, it had evidently not eliminated the pride implicit in the experience (ch. 8: 1-2) or the evil source productive both of the idol and of the idolatry. Assuming that idols are nonentities, there is a source and a peculiar necessity that gives rise to them which is not eliminated by the recognition of them as nonentities. They have no existence. There are no beings corresponding to Aphrodite, Serapis, and Aesculapius, regardless of how lifelike their images may be. Nevertheless, there is a power or powers behind them different from what their worshipers believe or from what the " gnostic " liberals in the church at Corinth suspect. Thus, although Paul agrees that an idol has no real existence (ch. 8:4), he insists that pagans sacrifice to demons (ch. 10:20). Though his monotheism excludes the existence of a plurality of gods, it does not deny the existence of evil powers responsible for the nonentities known as idols. The latter are essentially lies — things put forward as gods which are no-gods; yet the denial of them as lies is not necessarily the denial of the source of the lies.

The problem is not unlike that encountered by modern analysts of ideological pretensions. They can see through everything on the basis of rational insight. Or, to find a closer parallel to the "gnostic" liberals in Corinth, they can see through everything on the basis of a religious dynamic and assume that their freedom is invulnerable, only to yield without a struggle to the powers productive of the pretensions that somehow escaped analysis. The fact that Paul's conception of demons is conditioned by his understanding of angelic powers does not change the essential nature of the problem. A form of Christian faith all too ready to accommodate itself to modern freedom of thought and fraternization — concerned to give idolatry a hearing — will be infiltrated as easily as a correspondingly liberal democracy that considers its freedom invulnerable to its ideological opponents. What a recent observer of the modern scene says of the rational, civilized man in his susceptibility to ideological appeal is probably just as true of the permissive Christian: "All that we can safely predict is that, if exposed long enough to tom-toms and the singing, every one of our philosophers would end by capering and howling with the savages." [29]

The question to which we return concerns the vulnerability of the freedom which the "gnostic" Christians in Corinth thought they could have regardless of its influence on the weaker brethren. It concerns not only the danger to the weaker brethren, against which Paul warns in the eighth chapter (vs. 7-13), but the danger to the "gnostics" themselves, against which he warns in the tenth chapter (vs. 6-12). In either case it pertains to the risk of destruction which for Paul has reference to the loss of eternal salvation (chs. 8:11; 10:10).

According to his analysis, the danger could be traced to the fact that such freedom was fundamentally loveless. This is evident from his sharp contrast between the knowledge that puffs up and love that builds up (ch. 8:1). It is also suggested by the proudly perfectionist quality of the knowledge claimed by some who did not yet know as they ought to have known (ch. 8:2). But it is chiefly suggested by the inconsiderate and irresponsible attitude toward the weaker brethren, whose eternal destiny meant nothing to those who exercised such freedom (ch. 8:11-12). The same attitude seems to have carried over into the false sacramentalism of ch. 10, in which Paul recognizes a freedom involving a desire for evil (v. 6) and which is implicit in the self-destructive nature of the pride associated with it (v. 12). As a freedom that bound itself to no one because it concerned itself for no one, it was oblivious to the destructive potency within itself, just as it was oblivious to its destructive influence on others.

Here it may be asked whether the destructiveness that qualified such freedom was not the secret by which it was possible to see through the idolatry and to recognize that an idol has no existence. A freedom that is potentially self-destructive may, in the process of destroying itself, dispose of its idols as one stage of the process. It can dispose of idolatrous form as the epitome of evil as if evil had thereby been transcended. But it has only disposed of its idols — not the destructive potency within itself. It has only seen through idolatry. It has not seen through itself. Similarly, the modern world — which in so many ways has disposed of the gods in the interest of secular freedom — has not disposed of the destructive potency within itself, of which nuclear war is only the externalized, historical symbol.

On this basis there was no difficulty in principle in the " gnostic " Christians' participation in the idol feasts in Corinth. For the freedom with which they participated was the same in spirit as that exhibited in the idol feasts. As a demonic power itself, or at least as a religion open to demonic power, it pertained to the same generative source. This will explain the peculiar syncretism that enabled the " gnostics " to unite with idolatry by virtue of the claim that having seen through it they no longer had anything to fear from it. It is the same spirit as that which sometimes motivates bold community or nation-wide religious mergers or common fronts. The claim is made that specific doctrines, forms of worship, traditions, and denominational loyalties are implicitly idolatrous, or at the least, merely emotional fixations that can be psychologically exorcised by a process of reconditioning. Accordingly, all that is considered necessary to effect the merger or common front, no matter how different the religion, is to see through it, and by not taking it seriously, to arrive at the point where it is possible to cooperate, and to achieve a degree of unity that strikes the public mind as progressive.

In contrast to such freedom, the weaker brethren in Corinth were partially justified in their exaggerated concern not to eat meat of any description. They had an appreciation of their vulnerability to the demonic which their more liberal-minded brethren did not have, even though their weakness was inexcusable and unnecessary. They knew there was a line that had to be drawn, even though they drew it sharply and fearfully. But for all that may be said in their favor, the weaker brethren were no more representative of Christian freedom from idolatry than were their " gnostic " brethren. For when they stressed in a defensive manner their freedom *from* meat, just as the " gnostics " in an aggressive manner stressed their freedom *for* it, the same false dichotomy was exemplified as in the previous chapters with respect to sexuality — the ascetics with their freedom *from*, and the libertines with their freedom *for*. Both represented defective forms of freedom and therefore different forms of vulnerability. The " gnostics " were trying to be free *for* meat without being free from it; the weaker brethren, free *from* it without being free *for* it. Both were representative of loveless freedoms that interfered with the gospel or that nullified the sense of mission — in the case of the former, a self-autonomy that deprived their outreach of evangelical concern; in the case of the latter, a fear of the demonic that paralyzed it.

Therefore, surprisingly enough, there was not much difference between the " gnostics " and the weaker brethren, in that the definitive point of their freedom *from* and freedom *for* — the point that gave the prepositions " from " and " for " their orientation — was essentially the same, viz., paganism. Each really had their eye upon it more than they realized, despite their espousal of a " pure " freedom, which in the one case was aggressive and in the other, defensive. This meant that neither had their eye upon Christ. As far as their freedom was concerned, whatever its form, he was not definitive of it. This was why both were so vulnerable.

XII

EVANGELICAL FREEDOM
9:16-23; 10:16-24

9 *For if I preach the gospel, that gives me no ground for boasting. For necessity is laid upon me. Woe to me if I do not preach the gospel!* [17] *For if I do this of my own will, I have a reward; but if not of my own will, I am entrusted with a commission.* [18] *What then is my reward? Just this: that in my preaching I may make the gospel free of charge, not making full use of my right in the gospel.*

[19] *For though I am free from all men, I have made myself a slave to all, that I might win the more.* [20] *To the Jews I became as a Jew, in order to win Jews; to those under the law I became as one under the law — though not being myself under the law — that I might win those under the law.* [21] *To those outside the law I became as one outside the law — not being without law toward God but under the law of Christ — that I might win those outside the law.* [22] *To the weak I became weak, that I might win the weak. I have become all things to all men, that I might by all means save some.* [23] *I do it all for the sake of the gospel, that I may share in its blessings.*

10 *The cup of blessing which we bless, is it not a participation in the blood of Christ? The bread which we break, is it not a participation in the body of Christ?* [17] *Because there is one loaf, we who are many are one body, for we all partake of the one bread.* [18] *Consider the practice of Israel; are not those who eat the sacrifices partners in the altar?* [19] *What do I imply then? That food offered to idols is anything, or that an idol is anything?* [20] *No, I imply that what pagans sacrifice they offer to demons and not to*

God. I do not want you to be partners with demons. [21] You can-not drink the cup of the Lord and the cup of demons. You cannot partake of the table of the Lord and the table of demons. [22] Shall we provoke the Lord to jealousy? Are we stronger than he?

23 " All things are lawful," but not all things are helpful. " All things are lawful," but not all things build up. [24] Let no one seek his own good, but the good of his neighbor.

The problem that has been emerging in the letter to this point concerns pure freedom as competitive of faith in Christ. The fact that it may be outwardly expressed as a self-affirming freedom *for,* or inwardly expressed as a self-negating freedom *from,* does not modify the problem. It is still pure freedom and the adjective " pure " refers to its peculiar un-restrictedness. Although particularly evident in the claim of the libertines that all things are lawful for the Christian (ch. 6:12), pure freedom was implicit in the chastity of the ascetics, the purity of whose loveless autonomy disrupted marriages and bethrothals.

In the case of the " gnostic " liberals it was a destructive potentiality as dangerous for them as for their weaker breth-ren. As a threat to their immediate moral and spiritual integ-rity, it was a threat to their eternal destiny. Its lovelessness was no lack of a quality relative to what other men possessed but of that ultimate concern which characterized the ministry of Christ. The " gnostic" liberals did not seem to care what ultimately happened to their weaker brethren or, presumably, to their pagan friends. The fearful possibility of being lost according to the Biblical understanding of spiritual defection meant nothing to them even when, as a result of their influ-ence upon him, one of their own was in danger of falling (ch. 8:11-13).

In sharp contrast to such expressions of pure freedom, Paul maintained that responsible freedom can only mean restricted freedom. In what resembles an interruption of the main theme of the section, or even a displacement of material, his ninth chapter provides a lengthy illustration from his ministry. It concerns his refusal of a stipend from the Corinthian congregation, which under normal circumstances he would have accepted. It parallels the case of the " gnostic " liberals in relation to the weaker brethren, with the latter now represented by those sensitive to his acceptance of financial support. There is no doubt in his mind of his right to such support, no hesitancy in his claim upon it as elemental to his vocation. It would enable him to devote the whole of his time to the ministry and have the utmost freedom for the work of the Lord. Beginning with the simplest precedent — the fact that an ox was allowed to eat of the grain he treads on the threshing floor — Paul therefore reminds the Corinthians that those employed at the Temple receive their food from the Temple, and those at the altar, their share of the sacrificial offerings. As if to leave no doubt in their minds, he declares that Christ himself has commanded that those who proclaim the gospel should receive their living by the gospel (ch. 9:9, 13-14).

But he has not insisted upon his right to it and therefore upon the fullest freedom it provides. Although he recognizes it as elemental to his calling, he has not interpreted it as pure freedom. He has not demanded it. In the situation in which he finds himself he recognizes that the prevalance of religious quackery has created such suspicion that the acceptance of support from the congregation would be misunderstood. He recognizes that there are weaker brethren who would suspect that he was more interested in money than in the gospel. The fact that he would rather refuse his stipend than offend them therefore contrasts sharply with the "gnostic" liberals, who insisted upon their freedom regardless of the risk. For him the communication of the gospel was too urgent and the lives of men too precious to indulge in such indiscriminate conduct. The intensity of his feeling at this point is at once indicated by his declaration that he would rather die than have it doubted that the proclamation of the gospel was the sole purpose of his ministry. So he chooses to earn his living, that he might make the gospel free of charge, not making full use of his right in the gospel (ch. 9:18). As such, his sacrifice is incomparably greater than that of the "gnostic" liberals, even if they had refrained from frequenting idol feasts for the sake of their weaker brethren. It concerns the hard, realistic fact of his livelihood — the sacrifice of something good which was recognized by Christ as rightfully his. Theirs was only an idolatrous pleasure of dangerous potentialities, which, strictly speaking, to surrender would have been no sacrifice at all.

The decisive consideration is that Paul limited his freedom out of a profound evangelical concern that characterized the whole of his ministry. It pertained to the one comprehensive purpose of his life — to win men for Christ. His refusal of a stipend was only an illustration of a whole pattern of adaptation. He became as a Jew to win Jews, as a Gentile to win Gentiles, as a weak man to win the weak. The scope of his sacrificial conduct is suggested by his familiar observation that he became all things to all men — with the purpose that he might by all means save some (ch. 9: 20-22).

The secret of his concern to win men for Christ, which prevented him from becoming all things to them in a questionable manner, was the obligation to which he so eloquently testifies in ch. 9:16: "For necessity is laid upon me. Woe to me if I do not preach the gospel!" To understand this obligation in relation to what Paul says of it in other places, both directly and indirectly, is to understand his whole conception of responsible freedom and of the kind of restriction that qualifies it as evangelical freedom. As a probable reference to his experience on the way to Damascus which radically changed his life, it would have its source in the call of Christ (Acts 9:6). The necessity laid upon him would be definitive not only of the urge to proclaim the gospel but of the restriction that such a call imposed upon him.

The importance of this reference is immediately apparent in the manner in which it illuminates I Cor. 9:19 and is in turn illuminated by it, with the latter indicative of the paradoxical nature of the freedom propounded by Paul: "For though I am free from all men, I have made myself a slave to all, that

I might win the more." The special significance of the paradoxical derives entirely from Christ as the definitive norm. Freedom *from* men means freedom *for* Christ — in the peculiar manner in which Paul is bound to him as his slave. But just because he is the slave of Christ he is thereby enabled to become a slave to men without becoming enslaved to them. In this respect he is free *for* them. Thus, the one freedom, which is indicative of separation *from*, and therefore is indicative ultimately of holiness, is cognate to the other freedom, which is indicative of separation unto (identification), and therefore is indicative ultimately of love.

There is a curious similarity between such freedom and that required for good relations between parent and child, teacher and pupil, counselor and client, and other comparable associations that must be marked in passing. A counselor, for instance, must be emotionally free *from* his client to be clinically free *for* him; otherwise the objectivity necessary for therapy will be obstructed. And the same pertains to the parent and child, the teacher and pupil, in a somewhat different context. But in any of these paradoxical relationships which are necessary for wholesome living the crucial question will always concern the validity of freedom in either direction. Is the counselor free *from* his client and therefore free *for* him in a valid manner? Is the fact that he is free *from* him only in relation to his own objectivity, as scientifically or clinically understood, sufficiently definitive of his freedom *for* him? Is it sufficiently definitive of a freedom that must be responsible if the counselor is to maintain his vocational integrity? If such responsible freedom is restricted freedom, what precisely is it that restricts? What norm or law operates to protect the freedom from itself, either in the counselor or in the client, in order that it may be creative rather than destructive? Is the transcendence of faith in God required for such a purpose?

If we examine the peculiar obligation by which Paul's freedom was restricted, we will see that for him the transcendence of faith in God would be required for such a purpose. The necessity laid upon him that comes of hearing the call of the transcendent God in Jesus Christ constitutes the limitation by which freedom becomes truly responsible and creative (cf. II Cor. 5:17-20). What this meant for Paul pertains to his peculiar awareness of God's knowledge of him, in which God himself is the subject of the knowing. It was a knowing that bound him to God — a knowing that meant that he was chosen of God,[30] and most significant, that he was loved of God and enabled to love in a correspondingly new and creative manner. Thus, in Rom. 8:28 we find Paul identifying those who love God as those who are called of him. Similarly in I Cor. 8:3, at the beginning of the section on meats consecrated to idols and therefore in the context of Paul's consideration of the problem of freedom, love is especially designated as a consequence of such knowing: "But if one loves God, one is known by him." Since this seems the preferable rendering in parallel with the meaning of Paul's other references to God as the subject of the knowing (I Cor. 13:12b; Gal. 4:9; Phil. 3:12), love may be considered as the characteristic response to the necessity laid upon him. At the same time, such necessity in its determinative power is but the call of God in love that binds a man to him as love always does. This call concerns the activity of God that Paul describes as the divine searching of the human heart — not a searching to know more about a man but an activity by which God relates himself to a man, in the secret center of his life, as one who loves (I Cor. 2:10). In what is probably an amplification of the same idea, it is the activity of the Holy Spirit who pours the love of God into our hearts (Rom. 5:5). If, therefore, we are cognizant of the strong and persistent emphasis that Paul places upon such love as definitive of God's knowing of him and of his evangelical obligation, we shall not misunderstand the compulsive nature of his words, "Woe to me if I do not preach the gospel!" The compulsion is not derivative of the self-autonomy of pure freedom but of a love possessed of ultimate concern.

Such an interpretation of the obligation by which Paul's freedom was restricted and therefore rendered responsible is consistent with his statement of principle, in I Cor. 6:12 and

10:23, that all things are lawful but that all are not helpful. What he means by things not helpful may be found in the explanatory parallel in the latter part of ch. 10:23, where he says that not all things build up (*oikodomei*). This indicates that the things not helpful are things which fail to build up. And since from ch. 8:1 we learn that love (*agapē*) builds up, it is obvious that the things which fail to build up are the things uninspired by love. The factor delimiting freedom is clearly love, which means that all things are lawful within the limits of love — that love which comes of being known of him and therefore called. In a word, the limitation of the fearfully irrational and destructive possibilities of man's quest for pure freedom — a limitation equivalent to the transformation of pure freedom into responsible freedom — is the power of such love. With this observation it is but a short step to the identification of love with law, which is implicit in Paul's axiomatic recognition that love is the fulfillment of the law (Gal. 5:14; Rom. 13:10). Since Christ is definitive of such love, he is definitive of the law and therefore of the obligation that determines the nature of evangelical responsibility. For all responsibility involves a peculiar binding of one person to another. But here this is uniquely so, because it pertains to that binding to God which binds one to others in ultimate concern for them.

In this respect, Paul's understanding of evangelical responsibility is covenantal. It pertains to the manner in which God chooses a man (a people) out of the world for the sake of the world, which, as his elective action, is characteristic both of the old covenant and of the new. Such action is not inconsistent with the contractual nature of covenant, if we recognize how it establishes human responsibility and thereby enables a man to enter into a saving relationship with God. No covenant between God and man is ever purely unilateral or bilateral according to the simple meaning of these relationships. It is always uniquely both. With this qualification, it can be said that God's elective action creates a community in which men are freed from one another (free agents) in such a manner that they assume responsibility for one another and are bound together as one. A pure freedom of independent agents each concerned only to exploit the other, or organized into groups to achieve this purpose more effectively and therefore lacking in that responsibility for others which preserves true freedom, is a denial of the divine covenant. Similarly, a pure freedom of dependent agents, each concerned only to conform to, and to be absorbed into, society, and to identify himself with it completely, out of a desire to find freedom in its freedom, is equally lacking in responsibility and is likewise a denial of the divine covenant. A church of either description — individualistic or totalitarian — is only a religious expression of the same denial.

Such evangelical responsibility, with its presupposition of the covenantal community, provides the context in which to understand Paul's warning against the " gnostic " liberals, who thought nothing of entering a pagan temple and eating at the idol's table. The warning comes in the familiar passage I Cor. 10:16-24, which is the culmination of Paul's long treatment of the contentious question of meat consecrated to idols: "Therefore, my beloved, shun the worship of idols. . . . You cannot drink the cup of the Lord and the cup of demons. You cannot partake of the table of the Lord and the table of demons " (vs. 14, 21). In the context of evangelical responsibility the significance of this warning becomes clearer. We begin to see the deeper reason why the cup of the Lord was incompatible with the cup of demons, and the table of the Lord incompatible with the table of demons. The incompatibility does not lie on the surface, where it is obvious to all, as if the idol's cup and table were labeled " demonic " and syncretism advertised as dangerous. It derives instead from the total character of the obligation to Christ as Paul had known and experienced it. When Christ claimed him, he claimed him totally, with nothing left for an idol competitor, no further domain for such competitive sovereignty. It was this that the " gnostic " liberals did not understand. They seem to have viewed the Sacrament as an added protection of their pure freedom, as a means of safeguarding them from the danger that might accrue from it. Theirs was the same freedom as that of the libertines to whom Paul spoke in ch. 6:12-20. The libertines had failed to see that freedom from law means freedom for Christ, and never freedom to do as they like in his name (chs. 6:12; 10:23). The only difference between the " gnostic " liberals and the libertines, if one may judge from the opening section of ch. 10 (vs. 1-12), would seem to be that the former thought it safe enough to do what they liked in his name provided they had first taken the Sacrament.

But Paul knew that the total claim of Christ forbade this understanding of the Sacrament. For as he indicated in ch. 6:16-17, when the believer is united to Christ he becomes one spirit with him, just as in marriage husband and wife become one. A believer can no more take the cup of demons than a husband can take a prostitute. For the unity definitive of marriage, as of faith, pertains to the totality of life and is therefore characterized as an unconditional unity. It has a quality of " onceness " about it that means " this one " and " no other," as signified both by monogamy and by the fact that the believer is baptized only once. In fact, to emphasize the quality of " onceness " and therefore of its irreversibility, Paul in Romans uses the analogy of death as representative of baptism: " We were buried therefore with him by baptism unto death, so that as Christ was raised from the dead by the glory of the Father we too might walk in newness of life " (Rom. 6:4). There is a parallel here, it would seem, between marriage and baptism — the husband's dying as it were to other women to enter into a joyful relationship with his wife parallels the believer's dying with Christ to the old self and being raised with him into newness of life. What is observed here with respect to baptism holds also with respect to the cup and the table of the Lord, which is the focus of Paul's attention in I Cor. 10:16-24. The identification of the believer with the crucifixion and resurrection of Christ as creative of faith is definitive of the continuance of faith, represented by the repetitive character of the cup and the table. To drink the cup and partake of the table in the true and essential meaning of the act is to be crucified and raised with Christ in such a manner as to confirm and fulfill the same act which was originally definitive of baptism.[31] It is to realize that maturity which in Paul's conception of the Christian life distinguishes the believer from a babe in Christ. In either case, as Baptism or as the Supper, the act is covenantal, a genuine action of God (revelation), in which he binds the believer to himself through Christ. At the same time, it is a genuine response of the believer, in which he binds himself to God. As a covenantal pledge, possible through the grace of God, such a response recalls the classical meaning of the *sacramentum* as a military oath of allegiance. In either case the covenantal act presupposes the covenantal community, inasmuch as the peculiar binding of the believer to God is always at the same time an equally peculiar binding of the believer to other believers in the creation of such a community. In a word, it is creative of the koinonia.[32]

In the controversial text I Cor. 10:16, we see how Paul places the emphasis upon koinonia. " The cup of blessing which we bless, is it not a koinonia in [of] the blood of Christ? The bread which we break, is it not a koinonia in [of] the body of Christ? " The emphasis on koinonia is indicated by the word order in each rhetorical question, as well as by the parallel emphasis on koinonoi (partners) in the altar according to the practice in Israel (v. 18). The nature of the koinonia, as we have already contended, is determined by the peculiar identification of the believer with the crucifixion and resurrection of Christ. To have koinonia with him is to be crucified and raised with him, which in turn indicates what it means to have koinonia with other believers. It is both individualistic (freedom from) and corporate (freedom for).

This is not inconsistent with the meaning of koinonia, in ch. 10:16, as a sharing together in the blood and body of Christ. Even the idea of participation in his blood and body could carry this connotation of involvement in his crucifixion and resurrection, with the emphasis on action. There would be no question of participation in the blood and body of Christ in terms of a philosophy of being. It could be urged, perhaps, that the koinonia in (of) the blood of Christ corresponds to the idea of being crucified *with*, whereas the koinonia in (of) the body of Christ corresponds to the idea of being raised *with* — this as the explanation of the cup's preceding the bread. But apart from such an interpretation, the positive aspect of the blood and body of Christ as life-giving power, as well as the implicitly forward-looking perspective of their celebration (cf. ch. 11:26), would be enough to sustain the conception of resurrection with. The inclusion of it in Paul's conception of baptism (Rom. 6:4) would further support this view.

On this basis the koinonia would be a veritable covenanting in the blood and body of Christ. It would be the appropriate communal response in view of Paul's declaration that the cup is the new covenant in Christ's blood (I Cor. 11:25). It would correspond to the fact that his description of the sacrifice of Christ as that of the Paschal Lamb (ch. 5:7) endows the cup and table with covenantal significance.[33] In this capacity it would mean the creation of evangelical responsibility binding believers together in one body (ch. 10:17), each concerned for the eternal salvation of the others, and beyond the community of faith, for the salvation of mankind. Should there be no creation of evangelical responsibility, no resultant consciousness of mission, no awareness of the ultimate necessity that moved Paul to cry, " Woe to me if I do not preach the gospel," there would be no valid koinonia in (of) the blood and body of Christ. The lack of agape that Paul so clearly recognized as absent in the " gnostic " liberals would have emptied it of significance.

XIII

THE STATUS OF WOMEN
11:2-16

11 *I commend you because you remember me in everything and maintain the traditions even as I have delivered them to you. ⁸ But I want you to understand that the head of every man is Christ, the head of a woman is her husband, and the head of Christ is God. ⁴ Any man who prays or prophesies with his head covered dishonors his head, ⁵ but any woman who prays or prophesies with her head unveiled dishonors her head — it is the same as if her head were shaven. ⁶ For if a woman will not veil herself, then she should cut off her hair; but if it is disgraceful for a woman to be shorn or shaven, let her wear a veil. ⁷ For a man ought not to cover his head, since he is the image and glory of God; but woman is the glory of man. ⁸ (For man was not made from woman, but woman from man. ⁹ Neither was man created for woman, but woman for man.) ¹⁰ That is why a woman ought to have a veil on her head, because of the angels. ¹¹ (Nevertheless, in the Lord woman is not independent of man nor man of woman; ¹² for as woman was made from man, so man is now born of woman. And all things are from God.) ¹³ Judge for yourselves; is it proper for a woman to pray to God with her head uncovered? ¹⁴ Does not nature itself teach you that for a man to wear long hair is degrading to him, ¹⁵ but if a woman has long hair, it is her pride? For her hair is given to her for a covering. ¹⁶ If any one is disposed to be contentious, we recognize no other practice, nor do the churches of God.*

Certain women within the Corinthian church were defying tradition by dispensing with the customary covering for their heads. Their unconventional conduct was evidently an expression of the freedom they associated with the Christian faith and felt they had in Christ. The specific occasion on which they chose to display their uncovered heads was at worship, which indicates that they considered their action as having religious significance. Within this context it was undoubtedly an assertion of feminine freedom. There is no hint that they did it in public and thus by a form of conduct typical only of immoral women of the street were bringing discredit upon the church. The evidence associates their conduct with worship, particularly with praying and prophesying (ch. 11:4-5).

The point at issue was that the covered head symbolical of their subordination to men under the patriarchal order was no longer recognized by them under the circumstances of worship. In this they differed from Paul, who, if he recognized the right of women under the inspiration of the Holy Spirit to speak in church as an exception to the silence he otherwise imposed upon them (ch. 14:34), did not excuse them from covering their heads. He did not recognize that even the gift of prayer and prophecy freed them from their subordination to men. Why the women differed from him in his view that the inspiration of the Holy Spirit did not free them from such subordination is nowhere suggested. The reason can only be conjectured on the basis of those tendencies which contributed to the examples of irresponsible freedom in the previous chapters, viz., gnostic tendencies. These could have encouraged the women in the belief that their religious experience (*gnōsis*) was a genuine inspiration of God and that it freed them from the fleshly distinction of sex that an evil demiurge creator had imposed upon them. By lifting them above the distinction into the realm of the esoteric, it would thereby nullify the subordination. As asexual *pneumatikoi* they would be on the same level as men similarly divested of sexuality.

Whatever the reason for their action, the quality of treatment which Paul accorded the issue is not on the same level as that of his treatment of other issues in the letter. The peculiarity of his arguments, including his final appeal to custom or nature, does not reflect the Paul who in the high points of doctrinal interpretation exhibits the richest evangelical insight. The extremity of tone suggests an urgency to be met more than an issue to be clarified. The first peculiarity is his insistence upon a hierarchy of authority — God, Christ, husband, wife — which leaves us wondering about the role of the husband as an intermediary between Christ and his wife (ch. 11:3). Even if it means that the wife should be subject to her husband as the church is to Christ, and that the husband should love his wife as Christ loved the church, and should give himself up for her, how literally should these analogies be understood? Should the interrelationship between husband and wife be as similar as possible to that between Christ and the church? Should it include, moreover, what Paul says later in the letter about the imposition of silence on women in church, who, if they wish to know anything, should ask their husbands at home? How does such silence derive from the analogies?

Another peculiarity of argument appears in Paul's distinction between the man as the image and glory of God, and the woman as only the glory of man (ch. 11:7). The reference presupposes the Genesis account of the woman made of the rib from Adam's side (Gen. 2:21-23), in which, of course, no mention is made of the man as the image of God. This mention occurs in the earlier Genesis account (Gen. 1:26-28), where it is not the man only who is the image of God, but both the man and the woman together. The possibility that the Pauline interpretation is colored, at this point, by subsequent Rabbinic theology must therefore be recognized.

A puzzling turn in the argument appears in Paul's warning that a woman should cover her head because of the angels (I Cor. 11:10). Whether this refers to benevolent angels who, according to the accepted opinion of the time, would be present at public worship and therefore shocked at such immodesty, or to less benevolent angels who would be tempted to seduce the woman after the manner of the fallen angels attracted by the daughters of men, is not clear. At any rate, both interpretations rest on the same assumption — that women, contrasted with men, stand in a more vulnerable relationship to the angels.

But this peculiar argument is followed by another that is equally peculiar, at least for Paul — an appeal to nature or custom (ch. 11:14-15). He argues that the wearing of long hair by the woman is designed by nature or custom to show that her head should be covered. Without realizing that the opposite conclusion would be equally valid — that long hair is already a sufficient covering — he insists on the additional covering which the particular article of dress in question would provide. At this point Paul's patience seems to come to an end, so that he terminates the discussion in an arbitrary manner by simply saying, " If any one is disposed to be contentious, we recognize no other practice, nor do the churches of God " (ch. 11:16).

The impression that emerges from this curious complex of arguments is that the freedom affirmed by the women, which called into question their subordination to men under the patriarchal order, was particularly disturbing to Paul. To explain it as his reaction to possibly gnostic tendencies is inadequate because it fails to tell us why he was more arbitrary with these women than with those of the previous chapters, whose problems were ostensibly gnostic in origin. The women may very well have exhibited gnostic tendencies, but these in turn may have touched a sensitive nerve in Paul's spiritual constitution which made him react with greater vigor than he ordinarily would have. At any rate it is probable that he saw this assertion of feminine freedom as a fundamental revolt against the social order, which, at least in the eschatological perspective of ch. 7, would be unnecessary.

But much as he opposed the women whose action could have been the beginning of a feminist movement apart from gnosticism, he had in a measure encouraged them by his evangelical affirmation of freedom in Christ. For side by side with his insistence upon their subordination to men was his insistence upon an interdependence that implied a certain equality with men. On the one hand he says that the woman was made from man and for man — a clear reference to her subordination under the patriarchal order. On the other hand he says that man is now born of woman — a clear reference to the man's dependence upon her even under this order. Thus, in the Lord, as Paul explicitly states, the woman is not independent of the man nor the man of the woman (ch. 11:8-12).

The same juxtaposition of subordination and interdependence appears in the fifth chapter of Ephesians, in its Christological interpretation of the relation of husband and wife. Here the subordination is expressed in the clearest terms: " Wives, be subject to your husbands, as to the Lord. For the husband is the head of the wife as Christ is the head of the church. . . . As the church is subject to Christ, so let wives also be subject in everything to their husbands (Eph. 5:22-24). But their interdependence is equally emphasized: " Be subject to one another out of reverence for Christ. . . . Husbands, love your wives, as Christ loved the church and gave himself up for her. . . . Even so husbands should love their wives as their own bodies. . . . For no man ever hates his own flesh, but nourishes and cherishes it, as Christ does the church" (vs. 21, 25, 28-29). The Christological interpretation so highly developed in this passage, which, if not Pauline in authorship, elaborates the conception of the man-woman relationship implicit in his teaching, at once suggests the basis on which the women in Corinth could have claimed their freedom. They could have said that the subordination, understood in such a context of love, was no longer the same as the patriarchal order demanded, and for practical purposes was tantamount to equality. This conclusion would be strengthened if they appealed to the Galatian text, which says that in Christ Jesus there is neither male nor female (Gal. 3:28).

If, however, we examine the way in which Paul maintains a patriarchal subordination of the woman to the man even within his Christological understanding of their interdependence, an unresolved problem seems to remain. The subordination is derived not from the familiar answer previously given to irresponsible freedom: " All things are lawful but not all are helpful." It is derived mainly from extrabiblical traditions that occupy a place alongside the gospel, which is somewhat exceptional for Pauline theology. This place is not unlike that claimed for circumcision and the dietary laws by his opponents in the Galatian controversy. For instead of disposing of these traditions, as he did circumcision and the dietary laws, Paul makes them normative of the conduct of women alongside the gospel. In other words he seems to be clinging to a little of the law which, according to his argument in Galatians and Romans, should have been overcome. This is not to say that the women in Corinth were right and Paul wrong, only that his answer in the light of the gospel was as yet incomplete. It had been worked out for the problem of the Jew and Gentile but not yet for the male and the female or for the slave and the free.

The question which this will immediately prompt is: What were these traditions? What evidence do we have that Paul clung to them in spite of all that he said of the freedom which the believer has in the gospel? As the initial step in supplying the answer, we turn to his injunction of silence on women in church as we have it in the fourteenth chapter (vs. 34-35). Here we see that, much as his action may have been justified in the light of local circumstances, he expects of these Christian women what any rabbi would expect of Jewish women in an ancient synagogue. For although it was probably correct that the women in the Corinthian church were here indulging in ecstatic babbling, as Paul's use of the verb *laleō* (v. 34) suggests, and that for the sake of decency and order in worship they had to be restrained, the character of his injunction reflects Rabbinic practice. This comes out clearly in the brief, unobtrusive phrase that supplies the reason why women are not permitted to speak and should be subordinate. It is the phrase at the end of this thirty-fourth verse: "as even the law says." The law here in question is not the Pentateuch but the tradition that required women to be silent in the synagogues and that confined them to certain areas apart from the men, just as they were separate from men in the Temple.

It was this law which, if women desired to know anything, required them to ask their husbands at home — now taken by Paul from synagogue practice and applied to Christian women in Corinth.

But why this subordination of women? What is the reason for it? The firmness with which Paul insists upon it, particularly in ch. 11, in his peculiar complex of arguments culminating in an arbitrary prohibition of uncovered heads, makes one curious. His explicit injunctions that the wife be subject to the husband, much as they are Christologically qualified, makes one wonder how they are defined in practice. Is the silence imposed on Christian women, which required that they ask information of their husbands at home, an example of what it means to be subject to them as unto Christ? Is synagogue practice to be brought into the church under the caption of Christ?

For one of the underlying reasons for the subordination, we turn to I Tim. 2:14, where, apart from the question of authorship, light is thrown on what was probably germane to Paul's thinking. In this reference, emphasis is laid on the fact that it was Eve who was first deceived rather than Adam, and she who was therefore the transgressor. This, surprisingly enough, is the reason given for women not being permitted to teach, for their not being given authority over men, and for the requirement that they remain silent. It is the tradition of the greater inherent sinfulness of women, based upon the contention that Eve took the initiative in effecting the fall of man. The same tradition, as we see, explains the curious idea in I Tim. 2:15 that women can somehow make amends for this fact by diligence in childbearing — which, of course, obviously harmonizes with the masculine interests of a patriarchal order.

But even as beautiful a passage as Eph. 5:21-33 is not without the implication of the greater sinfulness of women. For even though the husband is exhorted to love his wife as Christ loved the church, the purpose served by it is that he might consecrate her as Christ the church, to be presented before him in splendor, without spot or wrinkle or any such thing, that she might be holy and without blemish (vs. 26-27). The question for us is, Why, within the Christological context of this beautiful passage, is there the one-sided emphasis on the benefits of the husband's love for his wife? What is there about her, in contrast to him, definitive of such a need?

The clearest Biblical representation of the greater inherent sinfulness of the woman appears in Lev., ch. 12, where the birth of a female child was twice as ceremonially contaminating as the birth of a male child. If a woman conceives and bears a male child, she shall be unclean seven days and continue the rites of purification thirty-three days. But if she bears a female child, she shall be unclean for fourteen days and continue the rites of purification sixty-six days. That such a tradition obtained at the time of Christ is clear from the reference to his mother's observing the rites of purification according to the law of Moses.

It would be wrong, however, to emphasize these examples to the point of exaggeration, because the theme they contain has no conspicuous place in the Bible. Both the Old and New Testaments are singularly free from texts and allusions derogatory to women, and just as free from speculation on the fall of man. These belong more to the late Judaism of the Hellenistic period, including Alexandrian and Rabbinic Judaism, and especially the Judaism of the apocryphal and pseudepigraphic sources. Here we find that the theme of the greater inherent sinfulness of women is more pronounced. As an indication of the change of atmosphere, an acrimonious remark of Jesus ben Sirach is illustrative: " From woman was the beginning of sin and because of her we all die." [34] Philo is more severe. In his allegorical interpretation of the Fall, the man represents the rational principle and the woman the sensory principle. The conviction of the woman's greater propensity for sin is unmistakable: " The woman, being imperfect and depraved by nature, made the beginning of sinning and prevaricating; but the man, as being the more excellent and perfect creature, was the first to set the example of blushing and of being ashamed, and indeed of every good feeling and action." [35]

A more extreme example, which appears in the literature of late Judaism, is the old theme of the woman's having had immoral relations with the serpent, so that the poison she derived from him was transmitted to the race. A Rabbinic version amends the interpretation in such a way that the corruption is removed from Israel by obedience to the law but remains in the Gentiles (Sabbath 146a).

In keeping with the spirit of these examples, Hillel (ca. 20 B.C.), whose name suggests the more liberal of the two schools of Pharisaism in the New Testament period, is credited with saying, "Many women, much witchcraft." But more representative because of its practical expression was the fact that the men of the synagogue of Paul's day regularly offered a prayer of thanksgiving to God that he had made them free, and not slaves or women. This, added to the restrictions that Jewish society imposed upon women, notwithstanding privileges for them that did not obtain in other societies, was neither conducive to feminine freedom nor complimentary to the feminine sex.[36]

The conception of the greater inherent sinfulness of women was not, however, incorporated into the theology of late Judaism in a consistent way, and so does not influence the main thrust of its doctrine of sin to any extent. In this respect Paul is not exceptional. His extrabiblical traditions relevant to women were not incorporated into his primary doctrines, even in his thought of Adam in relation to Christ, where, contrary to what we might expect, there is not even an allusion to Eve. These traditions lie, as it were, alongside his primary doctrines and alongside his gospel, unassimilated by them, so that his conception of women, as of slaves, is not essentially challenged. In other words, in his conception of women Paul's position is not essentially different from that of the Judaizers in the Galatian controversy in respect to Jews over against the Gentiles. Only substitute men for Jews, and women for Gentiles, and the similarity will be recognized.

The problem that emerges concerns the extent to which the

subordination of women, even within Paul's Christological interpretation, is justified. From the evidence reviewed, doubt has been expressed regarding the origin of such subordination, viz., its derivation from extrabiblical traditions. In other words, before the question of the place of women in the church can be answered we have to answer the prior question of whether we recognize the traditions that were mainly responsible for Paul's view of women. Are these traditions properly regarded as coming within the canon of Scripture? Or if they do come within the canon of Scripture, do they fall within the category of those things which are abrogated by the gospel? This latter question prompts another — one that makes us conscious that the whole matter of the place of women in the church depends upon our doctrine of Scripture: What are the things abrogated by the gospel, and how are they abrogated?

The issue cannot be evaded, as Calvin does, by playing down the high evangelical insight of Paul at his best in Gal. 3:28, where he says that in Christ Jesus there is neither Jew nor Greek, slave nor free, male nor female. For if with Calvin, who held the medieval conception of the subordination of women, and who lived in Europe at a time when many were still burned as witches, we say that Paul here means only Christ's spiritual kingdom — only what has to do with the mind and not with the outward relationships of mankind — then the argument of the letter to the Galatians respecting Jew and Gentile is undermined. For what Calvin says of male and female in Christ would apply with equal force to Jew and Gentile in Christ.[37]

But according to the argument of the letter, this was not what Paul meant. Both Jew and Gentile were to be reconciled in their actual, outward relationships as well as in spirit and mind. Circumcision was no longer compulsory. The dietary laws were no longer required. These significant religious rites which hitherto were of such an obligatory nature that they defined an order of things were shattered by the gospel. And it is the same for the slave and the free. The gospel is a power that shattered and continues to shatter slavery, not only as a spiritual and mental form of bondage but as an institution. And no less can be expected of that slavery which historically has been of greater scope and of much more serious and tragic consequences than the formal institution of slavery itself — the subordination of women to men. We cannot speak of the male and female in Christ, according to Gal. 3:28, as exceptional to what applies in the same text to Jew and Greek, slave and free. For if the latter are reconciled into one fellowship as equals by grace alone — a fellowship definitive of the church as the body of Christ — the same holds for male and female. The question cannot be evaded by arguing that the subordination of female to male is given in the natural order of things. For such an appeal — apart from the difficulty of defining the natural — would apply with equal force to Jew and Greek, slave and free. The continued subordination of one race to another — Negro to white, for example — or of slave to free, could be justified on the claim that it was given in the natural order of things.

What we have to consider, therefore, is whether in a Christological interpretation of the relation between male and female we should speak of subordination of the latter at all. For if the subordination is mutual, as Eph. 5:21 so clearly indicates in its exhortation to be subject one to the other, we should recognize it. To do otherwise, and on Rabbinic grounds for the sake of maintaining the legalistic authoritarianism of a patriarchal order, is to undercut the gospel. At this point, of course, most men will find it hard to surrender the last vestage of masculine pride which this order sustains and to see their relation to women governed exclusively by the gospel and its ethic of grace. Their masculine pride, confronted by the agape of the cross, will perhaps die a harder death than religious pride, which is represented by the righteousness of the law.

XIV

PROFANING THE LORD'S SUPPER
11:17-26

11 *But in the following instructions I do not commend you, because when you come together it is not for the better but for the worse.* [18] *For, in the first place, when you assemble as a church, I hear that there are divisions among you; and I partly believe it,* [19] *for there must be factions among you in order that those who are genuine among you may be recognized.* [20] *When you meet together, it is not the Lord's supper that you eat.* [21] *For in eating, each one goes ahead with his own meal, and one is hungry and another is drunk.* [22] *What! Do you not have houses to eat and drink in? Or do you despise the church of God and humiliate those who have nothing? What shall I say to you? Shall I commend you in this? No, I will not.*

[23] *For I received from the Lord what I also delivered to you, that the Lord Jesus on the night when he was betrayed took bread,* [24] *and when he had given thanks, he broke it, and said, "This is my body which is for you. Do this in remembrance of me."* [25] *In the same way also the cup, after supper, saying, "This cup is the new covenant in my blood. Do this, as often as you drink it, in remembrance of me."* [26] *For as often as you eat this bread and drink this cup, you proclaim the Lord's death until he comes.*

The incident presupposes the informality of Christians meeting together in private homes for worship at a time when they were dissociating themselves from the synagogue and were as yet without church lands and buildings. Their worship seems to have consisted of a fellowship meal, known as a love feast, which was associated in some manner with the celebration of the Sacrament. Voluntary contributions of food were provided by the worshipers, probably after the fashion of a modern congregational supper, with the rich bringing a larger share than the poor and the slaves probably none at all. In such an otherwise favorable atmosphere, extremes of conduct emerged that were typical of all that we have learned of the Corinthian church to this point, including Paul's description of it as largely recruited from the lower classes in the community (ch. 1:26). The love feast was desecrated by drunkenness, gluttony, and bad feeling, and with such discourtesy, particularly toward those unable to contribute (ch. 11:22), that the church was subject to further strife and division (v. 18). The revelry reached the proportions of a pagan feast and was probably responsible in the most literal manner for the weak and ill and the fatalities whom Paul regarded as signs of the judgment of God.

Such conduct anticipated the abuses which in the subsequent history of the church caused the love feast to fall into disrepute until it was finally discontinued in the fourth century. Abuses similar to those which desecrated it in Corinth were repeatedly condemned by the fathers of the church in the intervening centuries. In the interval of time separating the incident in Corinth from the letters of Jude and Second Peter, even more extreme abuses had arisen to obscure its reputation. Jude identifies the feast and those described as blemishes upon it who boldly caroused together, concerned only for themselves and whose conduct resembled the wild waves of the sea, casting up the foam of their shame (vs. 12-13). Second Peter speaks in a similar manner of those who were blots and blemishes, reveling in their dissipation — whose eyes were "full of adultery, insatiable for sin" (ch. 2:13-14).

Why the abuses should have arisen in the love feast at Corinth cannot be clearly established. Not enough is known of the origin of the feast to determine which of the various types of common meal peculiar to Greek, Jewish, and early Christian tradition was its antecedent, although the weight of probability would favor the latter. If it were the outcome of the table fellowship of Jesus with the poor, despised, and outcast, the abuses might be explained as those excesses which invariably arise when the church accepts the risk of identifying itself with people of this description (cf. I Cor. 1:26).[38] Since such free association was a fundamental characteristic of Jesus' ministry, in contrast to the religious exclusivism of his time, it would only seem natural that his followers would be sensitive to their evangelical obligation and continue the association in some form of common meal. If in the succeeding centuries the church was less willing to accept the risk, particularly after it was officially recognized under Constantine and became respectable, there would be less interest in those classes in Roman society whose poverty and degradation of spirit would incline them to the love feasts. If this was the case, the triumph of the tradition of the upper room would hardly be a triumph of evangelicalism.

If, however, as some contend, the love feast was a continuation of the postresurrection cultic meal, the abuses could be explained as a deterioration of the joy and thanksgiving that characterized it.[39] Any exaggeration of its buoyant atmosphere could easily result in the enthusiasm evident in the worship of the Corinthian church, inasmuch as the meal would have little or no significant emphasis on the death of Christ. Christ's death would have no more place than it seems to have had in those meals recorded chiefly in Luke-Acts, which constitute the principal source of our knowledge of the postresurrection meal. Without the discipline of an effective remembrance of his death, enthusiasm could degenerate into a licentious freedom.

It is doubtful, however, whether there is sufficient evidence to establish the fact that the Corinthians had participated in a cultic meal of this description. The abuses involved the desecration of a meal at which the crucified Lord was believed to be present and for which the Corinthians were held responsible. Since Paul speaks of having already delivered to them the tradition of the institution of the Sacrament, they were not unacquainted with it as a Sacrament of the death of Christ. Nor were they unacquainted with the gospel of the crucified Christ, preached to them not only by Paul but by his fellow apostles, who for this reason would probably not be unmindful of the corresponding sacramental tradition (ch. 1:23). Yet the Corinthians had made the meal an occasion of drunkenness and gluttony, and of such uncharitable conduct that Paul specifically charges them with profaning the body and blood of the Lord, in ch. 11:27, and of failing to discern the body of the Lord, in v. 29.

The probability, therefore, is that the abuses of the love feast derived from the same questionable spirituality and freedom responsible for most of the problems already considered in the letter. There is an obvious similarity, for example, between the irresponsible freedom of the " gnostic " liberals, who were devoid of concern for their weaker brethren, and the freedom of those who desecrated the love feast, who were devoid of concern for their poorer brethren. The drunkenness and gluttony with which they transformed the Lord's Table into the equivalent of an idol's table only illustrated from within the church the danger against which Paul had warned them from without, if they frequented pagan temples. Their action was reminiscent of Israel's apostasy to the golden calf, which Paul epitomizes with the familiar text, " The people sat down to eat and drink and rose up to dance."

More particularly, it would be the pride of the Corinthians, which was implicit in all their questionable spirituality and freedom, that would best explain their indifference to the Sacrament of the death of Christ. This would be consistent with what we saw in the earlier chapters, where the Corinthians resisted the crucified Christ as definitive of the fellowship they should have had with Paul, Apollos, and Cephas. In contrast to their glorying in men, Paul had decided in his preaching to know nothing among them but Christ crucified (ch. 2:2) and thus to lay the only foundation that could be laid for the upbuilding of faith (ch. 3:11). It was the same with most of the subsequent problems. To cleanse the church of the incestuous man, Paul had to remind them that Christ, their Paschal Lamb, had been sacrificed (ch. 5:7); to warn them against uniting themselves with prostitutes, he had to remind them that they were bought with a price (ch. 6:20); and to emphasize their responsibility to their weaker brethren, he had to remind them that the weak man was the brother for whom Christ died (ch. 8:11). In a similar manner they had to be reminded that the table of the Lord was the table of the crucified Lord. Without realizing this, they would misunderstand the table in the same manner in which they had misunderstood their ministers and had developed idolatrous attachments to them. Instead of glorying in men, they were glorying in the sacraments, with the same divisive results (cf. chs. 11:18-19 and 1:10-17).

Thus when Paul reminded the Corinthians of the original institution of the Sacrament, it was with the express purpose of not permitting them to escape the offense of the historical crucified Christ. It was to lay upon them an obligation of remembering Christ's death. This obligation can be understood only in the light of the whole situation in Corinth and of the extent to which the gospel of the cross was regarded as scandalous and foolish. This is the principal reason that it is necessary to insist upon the familiar rendering in ch. 11:24-25: " Do this in remembrance of me," and not as some contend: " Do this that God may remember me." [40] The latter would weaken the practical thrust of Paul's appeal. Paul addresses his emphatic words to those persons who are most in need of remembering the Crucified One — not to those who should " do this that God may remember," even though God's remembering is never merely an act of recollection.

What does it mean to eat the bread and drink the cup in remembrance of the death of Christ? Is the remembering a simple recollection of a past event, as one would commemorate the death of a great man whose memory was cherished? Is it a contemplation of the event with such dramatic effect that it seems to be happening before one's eyes? Is it an intensification of pity that prompts one to weep over him as the women wept over him on the way to the cross (Luke 23:27-28)? If these were the only possibilities, the remembering would be no more than the experience typical of the devotees of a mystery cult, who are capable of a frenzied contemplation of the sufferings of a mythical god. There would be no gospel in the remembering, no specific realization that it is not the death of Christ as death which is the focal point of significance, but the death of Christ as procuring deliverance from the bondage of guilt. The whole significance of the Pauline affirmation is that Christ died for our sins according to the Scriptures (I Cor. 15:3). In other words, the gospel is not a past event, even though the death of Christ, in which it is validated, is a past event historically speaking. Thus, to eat the bread and drink the cup is a reappropriation of the gospel, and as such, its proclamation within the fellowship of believers (ch. 11:26).

But since the gospel is not only a human word (sign), in all the depth and mystery and action of a genuine human word, but also the divine word, in a similar dimension of depth and mystery and action, what we have in the remembering is a reciprocal relationship of revelation and human witness. The gospel is a human word, but it is also the power of God unto salvation (Rom. 1:16). The human word is an attestation to, and also a communication of, the divine word, with the use of conventional symbols of various kinds (cf. I Thess. 2:13). The Sacrament is only another form of the gospel — the gospel as koinonia and therefore actualized in the lives of the people — and does not add anything essentially new or different to other forms of the gospel. In its sacramental form, which is its cultic form, it will have the same quality of offense as other forms, so that the sign in which the offense is communicated is not amenable to investigation. A science of signs as such simply means that for the purposes of investigation the offense has been eliminated. For the real Sacrament offends, so that any glorying in it, according to the flesh, is invalidated — only that glorying by which, in Pauline language, the world is crucified unto the worshiper and he unto the world is valid (Gal. 6:14).

The Sacrament as thus interpreted is essentially the revelation of the love of God, inasmuch as Paul always speaks of the death of Christ as essentially the manifestation of such love. Although it is correct to say that in baptism the believer is crucified and raised with Christ, and that in the Lord's Supper he is renewed in such a relationship with Christ, the action is to be understood primarily as one of love rather than of judgment.[41] Or, strictly speaking, it is to be understood as love inclusive of judgment and repentance — never as repentance legalistically understood and therefore self-initiated and self-imposed, and indicative of a continuing tyranny of self-judgment. For who is ever able to prepare himself for the Sacrament of the Lord's Supper (revelation)? Who ever arrives at the point of being good enough to come? Or, conversely, who is able to condemn himself to the point of being accepted apart from the love of Christ, which is concerned with neither goodness nor badness as self-initiated for such a purpose? The love revealed in the Sacrament is the same love of which such a representative text as Rom. 5:8 speaks: " God shows his love for us in that while we were yet sinners Christ died for us." The kerygmatic focus of such love in the institution of the Sacrament is to be found in the phrase " for you," the meaning of which is implied in the succeeding affirmation, " This cup is the new covenant in my blood " (I Cor. 11:25; cf. Mark 14:24: " poured out for many " ; Matt. 26:28: " poured out for many for the forgiveness of sins ").

The implication is that there can be no valid communion of the body and blood of Christ without the reality (revelation) of such love in the heart of the believer — not as a static reality but as an active reality, which involves reconciliation with fellow believers and as far as possible with all men (Rom. 12:16-18). This was implied in the previous interpretation of the Sacrament that God and the believer covenant together — an interpretation that need not be further elaborated here except to integrate it into the context of the discussion. Such love (agape) is covenantal love, which involves a mutual binding of God and men, and of men with one another into a covenantal community.[42] For this reason, what Christ said of the primary obligation of the worshiper in the Temple applies with equal seriousness to those who come to the Lord's Table. "If you are offering your gift at the altar, and there remember that your brother has something against you, leave your gift there before the altar and go; first be reconciled to your brother, and then come and offer your gift" (Matt. 5:23-24). Since the believer offers himself as his gift to God — "a living sacrifice [crucified with], holy and acceptable to God, which is [his] spiritual worship" — how much more should he leave this gift and be reconciled to his brother?

It will be understood why Paul was so profoundly disturbed by the extreme conduct associated with the love feast. Those who had indulged in it had not profaned the body and blood of the Lord as if these were isolated objects, but they had profaned the love represented by the phrase "for you," which gave the body and blood their evangelical significance. The body and blood of the Lord is what God has done in the death of Christ for the salvation of men. They are defined by his soteriological action. Unless this is recognized, they are easily misconceived as noumenal objects of superstition, which means, in the end, a nonevangelical understanding of the Sacrament. The bread and the wine come to be regarded as the loci of a static presence correlative with a philosophy of being and exclusive of any conception of being through action. This means that they are regarded as the loci of a "pure" presence (the so-called "real" presence) that is but the sacramental equivalent of the "pure" freedom considered in our previous discussion of meat consecrated to idols. "Pure" presence implies man's self-initiative, as suggested by the phraseology of those prayers which speak of the worshiper as coming into the presence of God. It excludes the possibility of the divine initiative definitive of the gospel and therefore the possibility of an evangelical understanding of communication. It eliminates the possibility of a presence in action — an action toward or away from the believer — which means that it eliminates love. As a consequence, a sacramental " pure " presence is just as loveless as "pure " freedom and therefore, insofar as it is definitive of the separation signified by holiness, is indicative of what is wrong with " holy " Communion.

These observations are particularly relevant to Paul's warning that whoever eats the bread and drinks the cup in an unworthy manner will be guilty of profaning the body and blood of the Lord (I Cor. 11:27) and of failing to discern the Lord's body (v. 29), thus bringing judgment upon himself. The way in which we interpret these verses will be indicative of our understanding of the abuses of the love feast and of the positive relation of the Sacrament to the total fellowship (koinonia) of the church. The exegetical controversy over the question of whether *sōma* in v. 29 means the Lord's body identified or associated in some sense with the elements on the table or with the church seems to arise only as a false alternative on the presupposition of a " pure " presence and the question of proper locale, which is always implicit in it. A covenantal conception of participation in the Sacrament, which involves the mutual action of God and worshiper, means that *sōma* refers both to the elements on the table and to the church, in each case as action. The imperative to the worshiper is to partake in remembrance of Christ. This partaking is a sign that is done, an acted parable, which is comparable to the Johannine conception of a *sēmeion* that is done, and the Marcan conception of *dynamis*.[43] Since the presence in action is mutual — the divine initiative toward the people and the response of the people toward God — the so-called " real " presence is in both phases of the action. Thus it is just as necessary to take with equal sacramental seriousness the fact that the people are the temple of the Holy Spirit (I Cor. 3:16; Rom. 8:10) as it is to take the elements as signifying the body and blood of Christ. In such a relational conception of action there is no less of a sacramental responsibility toward one's brother in the pew than toward the elements on the table, because Christ is no less present in the one than he is in the other.

On this basis a positive, evangelical relationship is established between the observance of the Sacrament and the total fellowship (koinonia) of the church. The two are integral to one another, so that when the latter is defined and determined by the former we have what is meant by a valid observance of the Sacrament. When, however, it comes to pass that the Sacrament is separated from the total fellowship (koinonia) of the church, either through abuses which make the two incompatible or through ecclesiastical arrangement as an alleged correction of the abuses, the latter is not defined and determined by the former. The latter tends to become secularized and therefore productive of abuses comparable to those which arose in ancient Corinth. This raises the question of whether the abolition of the love feast in the fourth century was an adequate solution of the underlying cause of the abuses. The persistence of the love feast into the fourth century would seem to indicate that it was a well-established practice and probably representative of a substantial human need. Paul nowhere condemned it or called for its abolition, but only for its reformation. The fact, moreover, that its somewhat secularized equivalent has reappeared in the modern church in the number and variety of common meals served under its auspices shows that the unsolved problem remains. The Lord's Table seems to have little or no relevance to these meals and is separated from them. As a result, the kitchen is so firmly established as a normal facility in the life and work of the church that for practical purposes the common meal is really definitive of the meaning of Christian fellowship. At this point the important question that emerges is whether its influences supplements the significance of the Lord's Table or competes with it. Is it only the actualization, in the lives of the people, of what is implicit in the fellowship (koinonia) of the body and blood of Christ, or is it an escape from Christ comparable to the manner in which men will eat when under the tension of what they do not wish to face, they find a certain compensatory pleasure in eating? Is it a contribution to that fellowship with others which is identical with bearing one's cross and following Christ, or is it a transmutation of

such a responsibility into something demonically facile that
never advances in seriousness beyond the rim of the coffee
cup? Doubtless, the emphasis which the cult of the kitchen
places on eating not infrequently reaches the point in the
modern church where the indulgence resembles that of the
ancient Corinthian church. The spectacle of those who can
eat together at the Lord's Table and the next day quarrel in
the church kitchen is too frequent to assume that the problem
in ancient Corinth has nothing to teach us or that it was solved
with the abolition of the love feast in the fourth century.

The essential reason that the ancient Corinthians profaned
the body and blood of the Lord consisted in the fact that
they were unrepentant and loveless. Their outward behavior
was indicative of this. They could come both to the love feast
and to the Sacrament with no agape in their heart. They
could come with ill will, prejudice, and hatred toward their
brethren, or with an indifference that was unconcerned even
if their brethren were destroyed. In this respect it was their
lovelessness that was definitive of their blasphemy. It was
their lovelessness that erupted in gluttony and drunkenness. In
their own way they thought they had fellowship of a kind, just
as the intemperate secular man may assume he has it in his club
or tavern although he is fundamentally loveless. Their superficial camaraderie was a far cry from the reconciliation of
Christ. They could take the Sacrament, and like the priest and
Levite in the parable, pass their brother by on the other side
without concern for his salvation. Profaning the Sacrament in
this respect is a denial of its purpose in the spiritual renewal
of the believer, which cannot take place merely between himself and God in the privacy of a mystical relationship but must
include his neighbor as he assumes evangelical responsibility
for him. On this basis it is perhaps not too much to claim that
the most serious profaning of the Sacrament is the manner in
which people may come to church and to the Lord's Table
as isolated individuals without recognizing or knowing one
another, and for practical purposes, devoid even of the most
elemental fellowship. It is merely accidental that they are in

the same building, attending the same service, and coming to the same table. This fragmentation of people into isolated, fundamentally lonely individuals for whom the fellowship of the Lord's Table is only a ceremony is essentially blasphemous. No increase in the frequency of the ceremony as such will solve the problem. For in coming to the table they are not really coming together, but each is eating by himself (cf. I Cor. 11:21) without discerning the Lord's body in the person of those complete strangers next to him in the pew, for whom he accepts no responsibility but who nevertheless are those for whom Christ died.

Profaning the Sacrament in this sense is the same as preventing it from contributing to the maturity of the church understood both individually and corporately. As the peculiar form of the gospel by which one believer witnesses to another by mutually covenanting in Christ, the Sacrament ministers to such maturity. The latter is a working out of his salvation in fear and trembling — an effective hearing of the gospel, which, as a babe in Christ, he did not previously have the ears to hear. The recent emphasis on the gospel as that which is to be proclaimed only to outsiders and not to the congregation — at least to the latter only once, in principle, after which they are taught — besides being grossly oversimplified, separates the gospel as deplorably from the Sacrament as it does from teaching. It subordinates the preaching of the gospel to the Sacrament in the same unfortunate manner that it subordinates teaching to preaching, in each case minimizing the unity of the three.[44]

The seriousness with which Paul viewed the conduct of those who desecrated the Sacrament is seen in his conclusion that the judgment of God had been visited upon them in the fact that many were weak and ill, and some had died. In such a conclusion he resumes a theme that has been integral to his thinking throughout the letter. It is parallel with what he says of the conduct of Israel in the wilderness when the people were guilty of desecrating the sacraments of Moses. With most of them, God was not pleased, for they were overthrown in the wilderness. Twenty-three thousand died in a single day and some died of poisonous serpents. They were destroyed by the Destroyer (ch. 10:1-10). In this instance the reference to the Destroyer, who presumably was the agent of judgment upon those guilty of profaning the body and blood of the Lord, recalls the discipline accorded the incestuous man. His deliverance to Satan for the destruction of the flesh that his spirit might be saved in the day of the Lord Jesus reveals a similar conception of judgment. In the case of both the incestuous man and of the desecration of the Sacrament we are reminded of Paul's earlier warning in the letter that if anyone destroys the temple of God, him will God destroy (ch. 3:17; cf. Rom. 12:19; Gal. 6:7-8). Since Paul identifies the temple of God with the people of the congregation themselves, the destruction of the temple is implicit in any lack of evangelical responsibility for one another — as illustrated by the lack of concern for the weaker brother or for the poor at the love feast.

The peculiar manner in which Paul conceived of the judgment of God is probably colored by the same contemporary idea of divine punishment that we saw in the case of the incestuous man. But it would be inconsistent with the revelation of God conceived as action not to recognize a corresponding form of judgment — the negative phase of such action. This will be different in quality from any conception of judgment based, in the legalistic sense, upon man's self-initiated, judgmental approach. But as the negative aspect of the divine initiative — man's negation of himself due to the fact that God cannot be other than the God of love he is and cannot accommodate to man's opposition — it is a more radical form of judgment than the inescapably arbitrary character of legalistic judgment. It is the ultimate and mysterious judgment that men bring upon themselves in rejecting and attempting to destroy the agape (love) of God. It is all that is meant by the perishing of those to whom the word of the cross is foolishness (ch. 1:18). If it seems strange that Paul should think of weakness, illness, and death as evidence of such judgment, we should not be prevented from recognizing that, in modern terms, the impoverishment of love, indeed the harboring of hate in the heart of man in any form, is its own worst judgment. In God's ordering of human life, such hatred, often so deep and subtle as to seem ineradicable, cannot be other than productive of weakness, sickness, and death in the most literal, psychosomatic sense. It takes its toll of human life on every hand. But where does it do so more disastrously than in the church when men who are confronted by the agape (love) of God in Christ profane it and thereby identify themselves with those who crucified him?

XV

RIVALRY OVER SPIRITUAL GIFTS, SERVICES, AND ACCOMPLISHMENTS

12:1-26

12 *Now concerning spiritual gifts, brethren, I do not want you to be uninformed.* [2] *You know that when you were heathen, you were led astray to dumb idols, however you may have been moved.* [3] *Therefore I want you to understand that no one speaking by the Spirit of God ever says "Jesus be cursed!" and no one can say "Jesus is Lord" except by the Holy Spirit.*

4 *Now there are varieties of gifts, but the same Spirit;* [5] *and there are varieties of service, but the same Lord;* [6] *and there are varieties of working, but it is the same God who inspires them all in every one.* [7] *To each is given the manifestation of the Spirit for the common good.* [8] *To one is given through the Spirit the utterance of wisdom, and to another the utterance of knowledge according to the same Spirit,* [9] *to another faith by the same Spirit, to another gifts of healing by the one Spirit,* [10] *to another the working of miracles, to another prophecy, to another the ability to distinguish between spirits, to another various kinds of tongues, to another the interpretation of tongues.* [11] *All these are inspired by one and the same Spirit, who apportions to each one individually as he wills.*

12 *For just as the body is one and has many members, and all the members of the body, though many, are one body, so it is with Christ.* [13] *For by one Spirit we were all baptized into one body — Jews or Greeks, slaves or free — and all were made to drink of one Spirit.*

14 *For the body does not consist of one member but of many.* [15] *If the foot should say, "Because I am not a hand, I do not be-*

153

long to the body," that would not make it any less a part of the body. [16] And if the ear should say, " Because I am not an eye, I do not belong to the body," that would not make it any less a part of the body. [17] If the whole body were an eye, where would be the hearing? If the whole body were an ear, where would be the sense of smell? [18] But as it is, God arranged the organs in the body, each one of them, as he chose. [19] If all were a single organ, where would the body be? [20] As it is, there are many parts, yet one body. [21] The eye cannot say to the hand, " I have no need of you," nor again the head to the feet, " I have no need of you." [22] On the contrary, the parts of the body which seem to be weaker are indispensable, [23] and those parts of the body which we think less honorable we invest with the greater honor, and our unpresentable parts are treated with greater modesty, [24] which our more presentable parts do not require. But God has so adjusted the body, giving the greater honor to the inferior part, [25] that there may be no discord in the body, but that the members may have the same care for one another. [26] If one member suffers, all suffer together; if one member is honored, all rejoice together.

The problem of freedom which emerged so clearly in the controversy over meat offered to idols and which before this was involved in most of the other problems of the letter now appears in the context of worship. It is not identified as such but may be recognized in the variety of undisciplined spirituality considered in chs. 11 to 14. It is first seen in the eagerness of some of the women to dispense with the veil, followed by the abuses associated with the love feast (ch. 11:1-22). But it is more vigorously expressed in the rivalry over spiritual gifts, services, and accomplishments, particularly the ecstatic power of speaking with tongues, which some of the Corinthians regarded as " the most exceptional and indeed the highest of the gifts of the Spirit." [45] The informality of worship typical of the house church permitted a surprising amount of latitude, with each person contributing a hymn, lesson, revelation, tongue, or interpretation. The variety and spontaneity of participation was indicative of a profound interest in the Spirit in the midst of all the problems which to this point in the letter might have persuaded us otherwise. It was not that the Corinthians were impelled simply by religious enthusiasm. They were " eager for manifestations of the Spirit " (ch. 14:12).

It is not improbable that Paul's recognition of the Spirit as " the giver of extraordinary and miraculous feats " [46] was susceptible to misunderstanding, particularly if the Corinthians thought that the Spirit was invariably manifested in the unusual. There was much in Paul that would encourage them in this respect. His preaching was " in demonstration of the Spirit and power " (ch. 2:4). His recognition of the gifts of the Spirit was broad enough to include speaking in tongues (ch. 14:5). His experience comprehended an abundance of revelations that would have over-elated him except for his thorn in the flesh (II Cor. 12:7). If the Corinthians seized upon this aspect of his testimony without realizing that, for him, manifestations of the Spirit were not necessarily unusual, they were provided with a precedent for an exaggerated emphasis on the ecstatic. This would be still more exaggerated if they failed to realize that the Spirit was primarily manifested in the confession of Jesus as Lord (I Cor. 12:3). If, moreover, their cultic meal was originally associated with the risen Christ rather than with the crucified Christ, it would provide a situation conducive to the ecstatic, as the tradition of the postresurrection appearances of Christ and the glossolalia of the primitive church (Acts, ch. 2) would indicate.

A somewhat exclusive emphasis on the Holy Spirit, separated from the gospel of the crucified Christ in what amounts to a non-Christological conception of the Spirit — a failure to recognize that the Lord is the Spirit (II Cor. 3:17) — invariably encourages ecstasy in worship. Of this tendency, the more strictly ordered churches, for good and proper reasons, have always been afraid. For although on the one hand the Holy Spirit is the quickening, creative Spirit, he can be understood as such only when he is the Spirit of Christ and not some other spirit. Being devoid of Christ is to be devoid of discipline, and ecstatic worship can thus become erratic and irresponsible, and inclined to deteriorate into chaos. In this context its potentially demonic character is sufficiently indicated by the confession, " Jesus be cursed! " (I Cor. 12:3).

But the solution is not to suppress all manifestations of the Spirit, particularly the extraordinary, because without these nothing essentially creative can possibly happen in the worship and work of the church. In this regard the extraordinary should not be equated merely with the ecstatic and the emotional but with the spontaneous and with those vital expressions of faith which are often unconventional, and embarrassing to the official mind of the church. If all is so thoroughly ordered and rationalized by liturgical casuistry, by rigidity of Scriptural principle, and by social and ecclesiastical control, evangelical freedom (paradoxical) is destroyed. No creativity is possible, and instead of the chaos of the ancient Corinthian church there is only an ordered, idolatrous security.

It is evident that Paul turned neither to the one alternative nor to the other. Although opposed to undisciplined expressions of spirituality, he did not completely suppress them. His avoidance of the one extreme did not presuppose the other any more than in the case of the sexual license of the libertines or of the irresponsible latitude of the " gnostic " liberals. Although he does not indicate as much, his norm seems to have been the same as it was in these two instances — all things are permissible but not all things are helpful, which means that spirituality must be limited in the interest of spirituality. The limitation is derived in the same manner — the identification of law with love, expressed in evangelical responsibility for the edification of the church (chs. 12:7; 14:12).

Thus, in the midst of his pastoral directive on matters of worship, which finds him recognizing the ecstatic gift of tongues on the one hand and providing a liturgy of the Sacrament on the other, appears his incomparable hymn of love in the thirteenth chapter. As a Christological definition of spirituality, which is at the same time the limitation of spirituality, it constitutes the liturgical norm by which all worship is to be judged. As the more excellent gift, without which all other gifts would lose their significance, it was the secret of the Sacrament as well as the explanation of why intelligible preaching was preferable to tongues. As the sign of the quickening Spirit of God, who is inseparable from Christ, it was the secret of that corporate unity which constituted the church.[47]

The problem came to a climax in the competitive atmosphere created by those who thought their spiritual gift, service, or accomplishment was the highest expression of spirituality and the surest evidence of the work of the Holy Spirit (ch. 12: 4-6). The list Paul provides — wisdom, knowledge, faith, healing, miracles, prophecy, discernment of spirits, tongues, and interpretation of tongues — indicates the variety of interest within which such rivalry arose as one or another expression was seized upon and emphasized exclusively (ch. 12:8-10). A comparable modern situation would be the variety of persuasion that often divides a church on what is most important in its services of worship, and beyond this, in the work of its ministry. Some become obsessed with music and emphasize it out of all proportion to the rest of the service, as if prayer and preaching were only of minor importance. Others are obsessed with the sacraments, others with prayer or evangelism or doctrine or tradition, as if their favorite expression of spirituality were for this reason of exclusive importance in the life of the church. But because it is relative only to personal preference and is promoted from this point of view, it is essentially divisive. However strong its religious appeal, it is not the inspiration of the Holy Spirit.

From Paul's account of the situation in Corinth it is evident that the rivalry relative to religious preference was a serious threat to the unity of the church. The same worldly wisdom previously identified as the source of the idolatrous loyalties seemed now to be determining the norms of spirituality. He who provided the gift, service, or accomplishment most highly approved by such wisdom would win the church's loyalty, not out of a genuine love for the person, but out of a vain desire that he validate its religious expression. The curious fact was that the preferences pertained to matters as good and necessary as wisdom, knowledge, and faith. But the difficulty arose when they were misconstrued as the peculiar possession of those who patronized them. Under these circumstances suspicion and jealousy soon emerged.

The destructive effects of a similar preference for what is good and necessary may be manifested in the life of a minister who adapts too readily to such a church. If to serve, and particularly to please, he attempts to fulfill the varied and conflicting expectations of its people, he risks the danger of breaking under the strain. In the acceptance of their confused conception of the ministry as normative of his spiritual life, he unwittingly incorporates their implicit divisiveness. Their rivalry in the context of the highest is accepted into himself and endangers his mental and spiritual integrity.

Over against the irresponsible freedom of religious preference in worship Paul emphasized that the diversity of gifts, services, and accomplishments all derived from a single source — the activity of the Holy Spirit. " All these," he says, " are inspired by one and the same Spirit, who apportions to each one individually as he will " (ch. 12:11). The character of this creative source, which is indicated by the confession that " Jesus is Lord " (ch. 12:3), imposes its own peculiar discipline upon the preferences. What this means is probably best represented by Paul's conception of the mature believer whose maturity derives from the action of the Holy Spirit in his heart, so that he now understands the gifts bestowed upon him by God (ch. 2:12). It pertains to that basic motivation and that creative insight which transcend the potentialities of the self as a consequence of the freedom exercised by God within the life of the individual. To use the analogy that best characterizes Paul's conception of such action, the preferences are crucified with Christ and raised with him — a result that recalls the phraseology of the Philippian letter, where they are counted as refuse for the incomparable joy of winning Christ and knowing the power of his resurrection (Phil. 3:8-11).

No one, of course, ever sacrifices his religious preferences under these circumstances without an agonizing experience of what it means to become a fool for Christ's sake that he may be wise (I Cor. 3:18). For no one in the deep, serious, evangelical meaning of the term ever likes to become a servant, offering all his gifts, services, and accomplishments to God and to his fellowmen " without money and without price " (Isa. 55:1). But when this happens in his life, the effect is similar to Paul's experience related in the third chapter, where his gift, in comparison to that of Apollos, is not productive of rivalry but of service and accomplishment in the name of the Lord: " I planted, Apollos watered, but God gave the growth. So neither he who plants nor he who waters is anything, but only God who gives the growth " (I Cor. 3:6-7). Such servitude as a consequence of the discipline of the Holy Spirit should not be understood after the analogy of worldly servitude but only as the servitude that comes of evangelical freedom (cf. ch. 9:19). As the motivational correlate of *sola gratia*, it is the freedom to love with that love so magnificently portrayed by Paul in the thirteenth chapter. As the answer to the problem of worship, it enables the believer to seek the unity of the church in response to that evangelical unity which is given in the confession of his faith in the crucified Christ.

The interpretation of such unity by means of the familiar conception of the body with its many members introduces a subject which in various respects will probably always remain as much a problem as it is an answer (ch. 12:12-26). Current theories of its origin are not sufficiently convincing to detract from the importance of the use Paul made of it insofar as this may be established from the text. It is evident from the trend of his argument, in which there is no allusion to its derivation, that his sole concern is to interpret the unity that belongs to the church as the koinonia (fellowship) of Christ. More particularly, it is to interpret the manner in which such unity comprehends diversity and preserves it. In this respect there is little doubt that Paul wished to avoid two extremes: (1) unity expressed as uniformity, in which the church would be an undifferentiated whole, and (2) diversity expressed as fragmentation, in which the church would be a dissociation of parts. The avoidance of either extreme is not a matter of finding a proper balance or a middle position between them (*via media*) but of finding the definitive source of the unity and diversity in Christ himself (ch. 12:12).

To avoid the former extreme, Paul emphasizes in the fourteenth verse that the body does not consist of one member but of many. Any doubt of his purpose is expelled in the nineteenth verse, in which he is explicit about the possibility he wishes to avoid: " If all were a single organ, where would the body be? " His emphasis on the many opposes any tendency to transform the membership of the church into a single type, apart from which all particularity of gifts, services, and accomplishments would disappear. The rhetorical questions at the end of the chapter are indicative of how insistent he is upon the maintenance of diversity within the church: " Are all apostles? Are all prophets? Are all teachers? Do all work miracles? Do all possess gifts of healing? Do all speak with tongues? " (ch. 12:29-30).

The effect of extreme uniformity upon the spiritual life of the church is to prevent the discovery and use of the gifts apportioned to each of its members individually by the Holy Spirit and therefore to thwart the contribution each would otherwise make. Such a condition obtains in the church when its ministry is characterized by a single, stereotyped pattern permissive of little specialization. It is associated with the impossible demand that all ministers fulfill the combined functions of apostles, prophets, teachers, workers of miracles, healers, ecstatic speakers, and interpreters of tongues. It also obtains where the opinion prevails that only in the ministry is it possible to render essential service to Christ, inasmuch as the laity are presumed to lack charismatic endowment. Or it obtains when the latter are unconcerned to discover and use the gifts of the Spirit because they have assumed that a contribution of money is all that Christ requires. As a result, the church tends to become an undifferentiated whole, possessed only of the unity characteristic of an amorphous constituency. As this happens, it becomes incapable not only of recognizing the gifts, services, and accomplishments of its members but of knowing how to use them. The inevitable consequence is a gradual decline in the quality of its leadership.

To avoid the other extreme, Paul emphasizes that the body with its many members is possessed of unity (ch. 12:12, 20). All its members, though many, are one body. With this emphasis, Paul opposes the fragmentation of the church into a number of isolated individuals, as if by virtue of belonging to Christ each could enjoy a private relationship with him without responsibility for the others. His fear of the possibility is reflected in the remark, " The eye cannot say to the hand, ' I have no need of you,' nor again the head to the feet, ' I have no need of you ' " (ch. 12:21). Such destructive diversity arises from the inclination of each to concentrate on the particular endowment of the Spirit apportioned to him, as if it were possessed by him or by the minority to which he belongs. As a false separatism characteristic of sectarianism or of a mystical privacy which presumes to pray and read the Scripture at home without identification with the church, it is equally characteristic of the specialist who is so devoted to his field that his objectivity isolates him from his brethren in Christ and disqualifies him as a churchman.

But perhaps the more serious form of such diversity is the isolation of individuals within the collective, as often happens in a worshiping congregation. " Each one has his business, his problems, his troubles, his hopes and fears, which he has neither the will nor the opportunity to share with his neighbor. In fact he does his best to conceal himself from his neighbor. . . . People open up to one another no more in church than they do anywhere else. They come in closed to one another and they go out closed. . . . In this respect the churches simply reflect the alienation of man from man which is the curse of our society. . . . People may speak to each other of the weather, business, politics, and even sometimes of religion! But they may not speak to each other as human beings." [48]

It may be observed that, in the latter part of the passage it-self (ch. 12:22-26), Paul's thought is controlled less by the body, with its many members, than by a sympathy for the victims of the rivalry disrupting the church. In the manner in which he speaks of the weaker, less honorable, unpresentable, inferior parts we detect a plea for those who in the previous sections of the letter have been identified as the weak, poor, foolish, low, and despised, whom God nevertheless has chosen. The compensatory interest in each, with the less honorable invested with greater honor, the unpresentable treated with greater modesty, speaks of the love which at every point in the letter has tended to break through to the surface. Although Paul's language pertains to the human body with its members, his thought now focuses less on their integration than on the love that binds believers together in Christ. For the fact that the transition to the theme of the thirteenth chapter has already begun in the twelfth chapter suggests that the significance of the body in ch. 12 is interpreted by the significance of the love in ch. 13.

Such an interpretation of Paul's conception of the body of Christ acquires further significance when the quality of love is recognized not only as that of the love revealed in Christ but as that of the love which the prophets came to regard as the basis of the covenant of God with Israel. This is best illustrated from the experience of Hosea, who " brought out overwhelmingly *the quite irrational power of love as the ultimate basis of the covenant relationship*, and by means of the unique dialectic of the concept of love illuminated the whole complex of the nation's history." [49] It is not to suggest that Paul was influenced directly or exclusively by Hosea, but that in his confrontation with Christ the love to which the prophets severally testified was profoundly illuminated. Such love, which may be characterized as the elective love of God because it defined his initiative in procuring the redemption of his people (Rom. 5:8; 8:28-39), is the love which in the thirteenth chapter interprets the significance of the body of Christ. Consequently, it is only natural to infer that the body of Christ is equivalent to the covenanted community, which would be consistent, moreover, with the fact that Paul conceived of the death of Christ as establishing the new covenant with the Israel of faith (Gal. 3:29; 6:16).

Apart from the probable semantic necessity of employing a conception as widely known in the Greco-Roman world as the multimembered body [50] to interpret the significance of the covenanted community, there would be the necessity of remembering that the latter is definitive of the former. The importance of this precaution is the protection it affords against reading the organismic connotation of the body-member conception into the meaning of the covenanted community, which is essentially interpersonal. Organismic wholeness always tends to absorb the individual and consequently to relieve him of his responsibility. It tends to dissolve the paradoxical character of responsible freedom by a one-sided emphasis on the identification of the individual with the whole, which compromises his freedom from it. Or if it recognizes such freedom, it fails to make adequate provision for it.[51]

This appears to be the principal weakness of the current theory of corporate personality as an interpretation of the ancient Hebrew totality concept or of the church as the body of Christ.[52] It provides no adequate explanation of why the individualism exemplified at best by the Hebrew prophets should ever have emerged from the totality — no adequate explanation of what Eichrodt calls " the antinomies of the unconditional ought." [53] Such unconditional responsibility of the individual pertains to his freedom " to represent that law of God which is over the people even by his opposition to the people and to see in this his call to personal service of the whole community." [54] The obvious parallel to such freedom, which we see in Paul as an individual opposing the Corinthian church for the sake of the church, is best understood, therefore, on the basis not of his supposed awareness of corporate personality but of his understanding of the covenanted community. This would adequately account for his conviction that the freedom of the individual for the community (unity) does not compromise his freedom from the community (diversity).[55]

Nevertheless the opposite is true — his freedom from does not compromise his freedom for, but deepens his awareness of the unity it represents. In this respect the interpretation of the body of Christ as the covenanted community has the possible advantage of deepening our insight into Paul's sensitivity to all divisiveness within the church. For insofar as the original psychology of the old covenanted community still obtained, it is probable that he would have shared the Hebrew aversion to any divisive threat to the community as a violation of the covenant. On this basis the greatest curse that could befall a man was that he be alone. The greatest blessing that could come upon him was a life of harmony with God and the community, as represented by the Hebrew " shālōm " (peace). With such a blessing transformed by Christ into the peace which passes all understanding (Phil. 4:7), Paul would be all the more persuaded that strife in the community was contrary to the nature of things.[56] As one for whom divisiveness was not, therefore, a relative matter to which a believer was obliged to adjust, he could only regard it as a sign of the greatest peril — the possibility of perishing. This would suggest the deep spiritual source of his concern for the Corinthian church.

XVI

THE SIGNIFICANCE OF AGAPE
13:1-13

13 *If I speak in the tongues of men and of angels, but have not love, I am a noisy gong or a clanging cymbal.* ² *And if I have prophetic powers, and understand all mysteries and all knowledge, and if I have all faith, so as to remove mountains, but have not love, I am nothing.* ³ *If I give away all I have, and if I deliver my body to be burned, but have not love, I gain nothing.*

4 Love is patient and kind; love is not jealous or boastful; ⁵ *it is not arrogant or rude. Love does not insist on its own way; it is not irritable or resentful;* ⁶ *it does not rejoice at wrong, but rejoices in the right.* ⁷ *Love bears all things, believes all things, hopes all things, endures all things.*

8 Love never ends; as for prophecies, they will pass away; as for tongues, they will cease; as for knowledge, it will pass away. ⁹ *For our knowledge is imperfect and our prophecy is imperfect;* ¹⁰ *but when the perfect comes, the imperfect will pass away.* ¹¹ *When I was a child, I spoke like a child, I thought like a child, I reasoned like a child; when I became a man, I gave up childish ways.* ¹² *For now we see in a mirror dimly, but then face to face. Now I know in part; then I shall understand fully, even as I have been fully understood.* ¹³ *So faith, hope, love abide, these three; but the greatest of these is love.*

The exquisite interpretation of agape that Paul provides in the thirteenth chapter is representative of a theme that threads its way through the letter from the beginning to the end. It is not an isolated theme that first appears in the thirteenth chap-

ter, but one that is interwoven with the witness which in every
section of the letter constitutes the Christological orientation
of Paul's pastoral directives. It comes to the surface only in the
thirteenth chapter, where it emerges as an epitome of evangelical beauty. The artistry there revealed is the artistry of
praise to God through which one beholds the grace of Christ
portrayed in the language of love. One does not ponder long
the unique quality of such love without realizing that it is
synonymous with Christ. His name could be substituted for
almost every reference to love in the chapter without distortion of meaning.

If it is less than evident, apart from the thirteenth chapter,
that the agape theme is fundamental to the theological thought
structure of the whole letter, this is largely explained by the
nature of the subject matter and the purpose Paul has in mind.
In the early section of the letter, where the agape theme is not
apparent, it is nevertheless implicit in the cross, so that the
offense of the one is the offense of the other. In the midsection,
the fact emerges that the discipline necessary for the preservation of genuine freedom is the discipline of agape. In the latter
section, as the theme finds its way to the surface, agape is characterized as the most excellent gift of the Holy Spirit. This
leads to the final affirmation of its eschatological significance
as correlative with the power of the resurrection. If it should
seem strange to conceive of agape under these four successive
captions as we move through the letter — cross, discipline, gift,
resurrection — this will suggest how much it differs from the
love which in common life and no less in religious life is so
frequently confused with it.

There is no doubt of the fact that agape is integral to the
significance of the death of Christ and of the gospel of the cross
which Paul proclaimed. This is sufficiently confirmed by the
classical passage in Romans from which emerges the familiar
Pauline affirmation that God shows his love (agape) for us in
that while we were yet sinners Christ died for us (ch. 5:8).
But the necessity of turning to Romans for verification only
emphasizes the extent to which Paul has been successful in the

early section of the letter in representing the blindness of men to agape as definitive of their sin. It was agape that was crucified on the cross and became a stumbling block to Jews and foolishness to Gentiles, just as it was agape that was incompatible with the popular criteria of divinity definitive of idolatrous loyalties to men.

Thus, the failure to recognize genuine deity was at the same time the failure to recognize genuine love. The reaction to the real God, who, when he appeared, differed so radically from popular conceptions of him that he was mistaken for a criminal and executed, was at the same time the reaction to genuine love. Such love was as different from popular conceptions of love as the crucified Christ was from popular conceptions of deity. It was not as the deceitful, degrading propaganda of the street, motion pictures, and magazines would have represented it — that love is easy and easy to learn, and that all are attracted by it — but quite the opposite. For truly to love is truly to live, and truly to live is to find eternal life. In most respects it requires a lifetime to learn the meaning of genuine love, which at once suggests that it is probably one of the most important and difficult obligations confronting the human being. No more revealing test of spirituality seems possible than the ability to recognize genuine love and to know how to accept and manifest it in daily life.

But there were others, for whom the crucified Christ was the power of God and the wisdom of God, who recognized that such power and wisdom manifested the love of God. The mature who had received such wisdom were those whom Paul characterized as possessed of the mind of Christ (I Cor. 2:16). This was an expression which in the Philippian letter related to the humility of Christ as the servant of God, obedient unto the death of the cross and exhibiting what we at once recognize as agape. The mature were those to whom the Spirit had revealed what no eye had seen, nor ear heard, nor the heart of man conceived. Presumably it was the agape of God which in this instance corresponded to the love they had toward him (I Cor. 2:9-10). It is in the description of the privation and persecution of the apostles to the point of becoming the refuse of the world and the offscouring of all things, however, that we detect more explicit evidence of agape. This is comparable in tone to the thirteenth chapter: " When reviled, we bless; when persecuted, we endure; when slandered, we try to conciliate " (ch. 4:12-13). The love that inspired these words has an obvious kinship with the love that is " patient and kind; . . . not irritable or resentful," and which " bears all things " and " endures all things " (ch. 13:4, 5, 7; cf. II Cor. 4:7-10).

The evidence for agape as a fundamental theme is still more explicit in the midsection of the letter. The behavior problems concentrated in this section, most of which are indicative of an erotic spirit, probably made this inevitable. No serious pastoral consideration of these problems — incest, litigation, relations with prostitutes, disruption of marriages, recourse to pagan religious festivals — could fail at some point to appeal directly to the love which all the participants so desperately needed. Such a variety of irresponsible freedom created a situation in which some form of control was urgently necessary. In the conception of freedom limited in the interest of freedom, agape emerged as the limiting factor and therefore as the basis of discipline. As previously stated, this may be inferred from the fact that those helpful things which limit freedom (I Cor. 6:12) are the things that build up (ch. 10:23), which in turn derive from agape (ch. 8:1). Agape is both freedom (Gal. 5:13) and that which limits freedom (I Cor. 10:23; cf. 8:13). But in the situation confronting him, Paul is more concerned with that which limits freedom and therefore with the manner in which agape is identical with law (cf. Gal. 5:14; Rom. 13:10). For this reason he is more concerned with agape as creative of that binding of the individual to Christ which is definitive of evangelical responsibility and which as discipline is illustrated by the concern of the mature believer for his weaker brother (I Cor. 8:13).

The surprise that may come of the possibility of agape as a basis of discipline will probably derive from two opposite posi-

tions on the nature of freedom, observed in the midsection of
the letter. The first has to do with the tendency of confusing
agape with permissive love. In this case the limitation agape imposes will be regarded as incompatible with love on the ground
that all limitation amounts to interference and deprivation, for
which the only appropriate response is anger. But since permissive love leads to indulgence and lawlessness, and to a deterioration of responsibility, it provokes a reaction. An ascetic
rigorism, which opposes all forms of love as a possible basis of
discipline, emerges as the opposite position. Its exponents react
against agape from a legalistic position as strongly as the exponents of permissive love react against it from an antinomian
position (cf. Gal. 5:6; I Cor. 6:15). None understands that
each is productive of the other, just as none understands that
agape can be the basis of discipline. For the one attempts to
discipline by means of its loveless limitation, the other by
means of its limitless love, which is equally loveless.

The transition to the third caption under which Paul considers agape, namely, the gift of God, begins with his observation that if one loves God, one is known by him (ch. 8:3).
This assures the recognition of agape as a work of God, and
agape is therefore less likely to be mistaken as a third factor between God and the believer which the latter can appropriate
for himself as his achievement (cf. ch. 3:7). What Paul meant
by God's knowledge of him in this instance seems identical
with the divine imperative laid upon him to preach the gospel
(ch. 9:16). Although representative of his apostolic commission, it was inseparable from that love for others which is always the dynamic of the gospel (cf. ch. 9:20-23), as it is of
the whole variety of gifts enumerated in the early part of the
twelfth chapter (vs. 8-11). A parallel in the second letter suggests the quality of the imperative as the transcendent power
of God, which belongs to God and not to Paul and his associates. As in I Cor. 4:11-13 it was the secret of their sustenance
when so many trials afflicted them (II Cor. 4:7-12). This
could scarcely be other than it was in Romans, where he was
confident that nothing could separate him from the agape of

God in Christ (ch. 8:38-39). In this respect we can regard agape as a gift of the Holy Spirit, and as Paul brings out so clearly at the end of I Cor., ch. 12, the more excellent way, without which all other gifts are in vain. As a gift it always remains a gift because only in this form can it qualify as the freedom that God takes within the life of the believer, apportioning to each as he wills (I Cor. 12:11). It is this aspect of agape — its identity with the activity of God, which we could equate with the grace of God — which we see emerging so clearly in the twelfth chapter. It is as though Paul had waited until this chapter to specify this characteristic of the contemporaneity of Christ and to bring it to light as his answer to the rivalry and divisiveness that has been the persistent problem throughout the letter. Over against the bewildering variety of religious perversity and activism which had come to a climax in a controversial concern over whose spirituality was the most important, he had to emphasize the activity of God, which determined the nature of agape as the gift of God.

The portrayal of agape in the thirteenth chapter, which Paul accomplishes with rare skill and beauty, seems to reflect three dimensions of meaning according to the arrangement of subject matter: the normality of agape (vs. 1-3), its stability (vs. 4-7), and its finality (vs. 8-13). In the first of these the vanity of various forms of loveless religion is exposed as each comes under the judgment of agape as its ultimate norm. The variety familiar to us in the twelfth chapter is presupposed as Paul looks outward upon the world at the variety of religion there. Without agape, each is empty. Each is insignificant, irrespective of the greatest sincerity and sacrifice: the gift of ecstatic utterance (v. 1), intelligible proclamation (v. 2), the experience of mysteries and gnosis (v. 2), wonder-working faith (v. 2), sacrificial humanitarianism (v. 3), and extreme asceticism (v. 3).

What Paul discerns is the implicit irrelevance of so much that passes for religion. All the expenditure of talent and effort causes the serious man to wonder in the end if it has not been a waste of time and essentially meaningless. At the center there seems to be lacking a reality that would give solid significance. The eloquence, the ritual, the mystery, the prodigious claims and sacrifice, have a fictitious quality, which, if not unrecognized, seems almost always unacknowledged. A deep, fundamental lovelessness, which at the same time is an equally subtle form of unbelief, seems to be the one, decisive factor creating the problem. This is not a lack of love in the various familiar connotations of eros ranging from sexuality to mystical, philosophical, and artistic expression. Nor is it a lack of love in the neurotic connotation of eros, as a desire to be acceped and liked and the subtle means of realizing such a desire through the art of winning friends and influencing people. All these belong to the side of loveless religion because they are essentially loveless forms of love, as devoid of agape as the wonder-working faith, the sacrificial humanitarianism, and the extreme asceticism which, according to Paul, had no ultimate significance (vs. 2-3).

The essential difference between the self-expressive, self-seeking, possessive, pleasure-principled eros-love, and that which Paul designates as agape-love, is that the latter originates in the activity by which God knows a man and creates such love in him. Thus, as we have previously indicated, Paul could say, " If one loves God, one is known by him " (ch. 8:3, cf. I John 4:19). The presupposition is that agape, as an unconditional, responsible, self-giving, liberating, creative love, has its origin not in man but in God. It is an expression of the grace of God and of the ethic of grace which is man's obedience in faith to him. The reason, therefore, that agape is definitive of normality in religion is that it derives from the revelation of God, whose knowing of man is a giving of himself in this extraordinary manner. As the love from beyond man, society, and nature which transcends the mysterious universe in its concern for man, it counts in relation to the ultimate as no other form of love or religion could possibly count. It overcomes the nothingness of loveless love and religion, which are not essentially different from nihilism. This is a nothingness before which love as an emotion or value counts no more than other human achievements that die with the individual, or with his generation or civilization, and are swallowed up in the oblivion of an ever-receding past. Without agape, what Ecclesiastes says of the supposed advantage of the wise man over the fool could be said of the lovable man over the unlovable: How dieth the one? Even as the other! What Paul means, therefore, by his insistence upon the normality of agape is its transcendence over death. As such it is the love by which and for which man was created and which in the purpose of God is natural to him. At the level of daily life, as agape defines the conduct of the community of faith, it defines what is normal to man, in contrast to which all forms of eros-love are expressions of his sin.[57]

The stability of agape is evident from positive statements of its patience and kindness (I Cor. 13:4) and its capacity to bear all things, believe all things, hope all things, endure all things (v. 7). A number of negative statements confirm this conclusion because they indicate that the qualities opposite agape are all qualities of instability: jealousy, boastfulness, rudeness, insistence on one's own way, irritableness, resentment, rejoicing at wrong (vs. 4-6). The list reads like a summary of the qualities that Paul has observed in all the forms of problematic behavior throughout the letter. At every point agape stands over against them in the stability it confers upon the man whose heart is open to it.

This second dimension of meaning is a natural consequence of the first. The stability of agape derives from its normality. For when a man is persuaded that nothing can separate him from the agape of God in Christ (Rom. 8:38-39), this anchorage at the center of his life, this normative confidence, gives him inner security and serenity. It frees him to love others and thereby stabilizes his relationships with them. Persuaded of the love which is living, active, objective, transcending the natural order, he knows that in such love, which is inseparable from the presence of God in Christ, his life and all that he does counts eternally. Nothing can detract from their significance. He does not need to be jealous, boastful, arrogant, rude, insistent upon his way, irritable, or resentful, because the insecurity that would give rise to these qualities has been overcome within him. For that which separated him from such love has been removed. He has experienced divine forgiveness.

The practical importance of this possibility will be enhanced by the observation of what happens to the individual when within the more immediate context of his family life, particularly as a child, he doubts the love of those nearest him. As a circumstance which, because of tension, division, unhappiness, and confusion in the home, is more damaging to him than those hardships and handicaps commonly regarded as serious disadvantages, it conditions his whole perspective on life. Although the love offered him is ostensibly love, it is essentially loveless love and therefore more damaging than no love at all. Its inconsistency is so provocative of conflict within him that his instability is worse than it would have been had he been subjected to consistent hatred. As an instability with obvious social consequences, it is correspondingly more disruptive of home and community life.[58]

The spiritual implication of such a traumatic effect of loveless love concerns the extent to which a similar observation could be made of the individual who doubts the love of God. As one who in relation to God is a child, it is not improbable that the effect of doubting God's love or being confused by the inconsistencies of life could be regarded as traumatic. Such a disturbance of personal life in relation to the ultimate could contribute to the instability of society. As more persons become convinced of the universe as infinitely empty they could despair of a love which, through its transcendence over death, would otherwise secure for men genuine personal significance. Under these circumstances they would find their precedent in the despair of Ecclesiastes, who, when confronted by a comparable emptiness, declared that he hated life (Eccl. 2:17). Such a possibility as the explanation of the enigmatic potentiality of human destructiveness in the modern world would at once suggest the enormity of the need of the agape of God as the ultimate source of stability.

But the stability that comes of agape is not a static stability. It is one which exists only in conflict, because eros-love continues as a sign of the flesh in contradiction to the activity of the Holy Spirit. As a love alien to agape, it involves one in that conflict (which Paul designates in Galatians) in which the desires of the flesh are opposed to those of the Spirit (ch. 5:17). Such conflict seems implicit in the contrast of the characteristics of agape, in I Cor. 13:4-7, with their opposites: patience as contrasted with irritability, and kindness with arrogance and rudeness. In each instance the characteristics are so clearly balanced against each other that the dynamic character of the stability of agape is at once suggested. It is the same stability as in the second letter, where in a passage descriptive of his conflict with the world Paul reaches the noblest heights of confessional courage: " We are afflicted in every way, but not crushed; perplexed, but not driven to despair; persecuted, but not forsaken; struck down, but not destroyed; always carrying in the body the death of Jesus, so that the life of Jesus may also be manifested in our bodies " (II Cor. 4:8-10).

What has been said of the normality and stability of agape will prepare us for the finality of agape (I Cor. 13:8-13). As its eschatological connotation, this finality is the dimension of meaning within which the normality and stability of agape find their proper definition. The stability of agape is qualified by the tension between an awareness of the present age as passing away and of the new age as coming with Christ (chs. 7:31; 15:50-52). The perspective has already been anticipated in the consideration of Paul's view of marriage. It is only necessary to associate it with the perspective that emerges in the latter part of the thirteenth chapter to understand how it conditions the meaning of agape. Here it is evident that prophecy, tongues, and knowledge, which are forms pertaining to the present age and which therefore pass away, are contrasted with agape, which never ends. This implies that the variety of religion that Paul associates with prophecy, tongues, and knowledge, and that would include all forms of loveless love, will disappear in the same manner, so that apart from agape's characterizing it, the new age will be religionless.

In his personal experience Paul had anticipated such an eschatological negation of religion in forsaking what he describes in Philippians as his confidence in the flesh — " circumcised on the eighth day, of the people of Israel, of the tribe of Benjamin, a Hebrew born of Hebrews; as to the law a Pharisee, as to zeal a persecutor of the church, as to righteousness under the law blameless." All of this he counted as refuse and left behind in coming to a knowledge of Christ. But with the thought of knowing Christ as he would in the day of resurrection, he is straining forward like a runner in a race, eager to reach the finish line and thus leaving behind even the temporalities pertaining to his Christian life (Phil. 3:4-11).

In Corinthians the same perspective is implied in his reference to prophecy, tongues, and knowledge as imperfections that will pass away and that are comparable only to childish things a man leaves behind on the attainment of maturity (13:9-11). The maturity of the man and, in contrast, the immaturity of the child, are eschatological allusions recalling the earlier distinction between babes in Christ and the mature. The eschatological perspective is obvious in the polarity of the Now and the Then which structures the passage and therefore qualifies the stability of agape as a stability within the tension between these two limits. The normality of agape is similarly qualified in that the same eschatological perspective is the test of religion — whether it passes away with the present world or carries across into the day of the resurrection and counts eternally.

In its eschatological significance, agape, like faith and hope, is said to abide but is affirmed as the greatest of the three. In this confidence Paul is not thinking of it as a quality or attribute which as a third factor may be abstracted from his relation to Christ and considered by itself. This possibility would only mean the transformation of agape into a category of the present perishing world. Instead, his anticipation of knowing Christ fully as the eschatological goal of his striving, which involves seeing him face to face and not as in a mirror dimly, indicates that agape is nothing other than Christ himself. It is the action of Christ in giving himself, and the corresponding action created in the heart of the believer by the Holy Spirit in response to him. The latter action is exemplified in Paul's striving to know him fully. In this respect agape is the fulfillment of the meaning of faith and hope — faith signifying the acceptance of Christ and hope as the anticipation of Christ. Both find their fulfillment in that final knowledge of him which agape signifies.[59]

XVII

THE PROBLEM OF ECSTATIC TONGUES
14:1-19

14 *Make love your aim, and earnestly desire the spiritual gifts, especially that you may prophesy.* ²*For one who speaks in a tongue speaks not to men but to God; for no one understands him, but he utters mysteries in the Spirit.* ³*On the other hand, he who prophesies speaks to men for their upbuilding and encouragement and consolation.* ⁴*He who speaks in a tongue edifies himself, but he who prophesies edifies the church.* ⁵*Now I want you all to speak in tongues, but even more to prophesy. He who prophesies is greater than he who speaks in tongues, unless some one interprets, so that the church may be edified.*

6 *Now, brethren, if I come to you speaking in tongues, how shall I benefit you unless I bring you some revelation or knowledge or prophecy or teaching?* ⁷*If even lifeless instruments, such as the flute or the harp, do not give distinct notes, how will any one know what is played?* ⁸*And if the bugle gives an indistinct sound, who will get ready for battle?* ⁹*So with yourselves; if you in a tongue utter speech that is not intelligible, how will any one know what is said? For you will be speaking into the air.* ¹⁰*There are doubtless many different languages in the world, and none is without meaning;* ¹¹*but if I do not know the meaning of the language, I shall be a foreigner to the speaker and the speaker a foreigner to me.* ¹²*So with yourselves; since you are eager for manifestations of the Spirit, strive to excel in building up the church.*

13 *Therefore, he who speaks in a tongue should pray for the power to interpret.* ¹⁴*For if I pray in a tongue, my spirit prays but my mind is unfruitful.* ¹⁵*What am I to do? I will pray with the*

*spirit and I will pray with the mind also; I will sing with the spirit
and I will sing with the mind also.* [16] *Otherwise, if you bless with
the spirit, how can any one in the position of an outsider say the
" Amen " to your thanksgiving when he does not know what you
are saying?* [17] *For you may give thanks well enough, but the other
man is not edified.* [18] *I thank God that I speak in tongues more
than you all;* [19] *nevertheless, in church I would rather speak five
words with my mind, in order to instruct others, than ten thousand words in a tongue.*

———

The most acute problem arising out of the rivalry over spiritual gifts was the phenomenon of speaking in tongues, which
was another expression of irresponsible freedom. It was not a
problem that belonged merely to the fringe of practical interest
and was therefore better ignored than publicized, but one that
engaged the attention of Paul as seriously as any other problem in the letter. Those who spoke with tongues were eager for
manifestations of the Spirit (ch. 14:12); they desired more explicit evidence of the power of God. Their motive undoubtedly arose from the conviction that the extraordinary —
particularly the extraordinary as a subjective experience —
was a sign of the Spirit. Having a subjective experience that
was a sign of the Spirit would enable them to appeal to their
own religious and miraculous power as proof of superior piety.

Speaking in tongues was a form of prayer (v. 14) that probably began with intelligible speech and by means of an intensification of feeling culminated in a series of incoherent, emotional utterances. Since prayer and song are often associated,
it could have begun with either one (v. 15). As a form of
speech which in some strange manner expressed the significance of what was happening within the individual, it was an
ecstatic phenomenon. It was prayer that had passed beyond
the point of the adequacy of normal language to express the
inner complexes of the soul, and that at such a stage seemed to
have taken control of the individual so that he was no longer
himself. To the outsider who witnessed the behavior, especially
when its contagious influence caught up others in the congre-

gation, it seemed like madness (v. 23). Its evident lack of agape was manifest in the confusion and self-involvement of each participant.

The irresponsible freedom, which is not unlike that exhibited in the midsection of the letter by the libertines and the " gnostic " liberals, suggests a gnostic tendency. The experience of ecstatic tongues, in which the worshiper is presumably possessed of the power of God or has his spirit merged with the divine Spirit, is the type of experience that could have been described as gnosis, and that in its effect upon the individual could have easily puffed him up with pride (ch. 8:1). As a version of the escape of the spirit from the body which, in modern terminology, would provide release from inward tension and conflict, it was scarcely calm and contemplative. A community as full of strife and division as the Corinthian church would undoubtedly have a subjective life of the same turbulent character. If a negative view of bodily life prevailed, the gnostic conception of the spiritual man as one alien to such a life would intensify the desire to escape. The alien character of static tongues would symbolize the process.

But apart from gnostic and psychological influences, the ecstasy of tongues may have been a legacy from the primitive church and the eschatological tradition connected with it. Evidence from The Acts of the Apostles specifically associates tongues with the gift of the Holy Spirit, constituting the church a catholic and eschatological community. The appeal is to the prophet Joel: " And in the last days it shall be, God declares, that I will pour out my Spirit upon all flesh, and your sons and your daughters shall prophesy, and your young men shall see visions, and your old men shall dream dreams; yea, and on my menservants and my maidservants in those days I will pour out my Spirit; and they shall prophesy " (Acts 2:17-18). It is the typical Jewish association of the Spirit with the Spirit of prophecy, as is probably the case in the secondary interpretation of the language as intelligible (ch. 2:8-11).[60] The similarity with the phenomenon at Corinth appears in the impression of some that the tongues were evidence of drunkenness, the importance of which is emphasized by the fact that Peter is at pains to deny it (ch. 2:15). This would mean that they were unintelligible. But whether intelligible or unintelligible, the fact that it was Peter's sermon which interpreted the event as a fulfillment of prophecy seems significant so far as a possible connection with the Corinthian church may be concerned. To what extent was this the kind of preaching that characterized his ministry at a later period in Corinth (I Cor. 1:12; 9:5; 15:5)? To what extent was he influential in creating an interest in tongues among the Corinthians? Paul himself undoubtedly believed in tongues, but not with the emphasis suggested in Peter's sermon.

Whatever the nature of the phenomenon, the probability is that in Corinth it was a complex of several factors and therefore not explicable solely in terms of psychology, gnosticism, eschatology, or the ecstasy within the primitive church. The gospel as Paul preached it was preached into a situation in which most, if not all, these factors were already present. In what peculiar combination we do not know. But whatever the phenomenon was, he was confident that the Spirit of God was also present, taking even the peculiarity of tongues and shaping it to his own ends.

It is significant that Paul neither condoned nor rejected speaking in tongues. Although he refused to give it a primary place, he did not reject it as wholly undesirable. As with other forms of spirituality, the crucial test was the manifestation of agape, without which it was comparable only to a noisy gong or a clanging cymbal. At best it was only an imperfection relative to a world that was passing away. It was one of those childish things which a man leaves behind at maturity. It was not a direct contact with the eternal, reached at what was probably assumed to be the summit of the soul's ascent. The significant fact is that Paul recognized the possibility of tongues as a source of edification to the person gifted in such a manner even though it was not a source of edification to others (I Cor. 14:4). Such recognition was undoubtedly due in part to his own experience of ecstasy, which included the gift of tongues (ch. 14:18; cf. II Cor. 12:2 ff.).

What he meant by the edification of the self is difficult to say. Previous references to edification have had a wider application. They have had to do with the consolidation of faith in love enriched by insight and by a quickened consciousness of evangelical responsibility. How the experience of tongues could achieve this in the life of the individual is nowhere indicated. But for Paul, who recognized the activity of the Holy Spirit within the heart (I Cor. 2:10; Rom. 5:5; 8:27), it could have reference to a cathartic effect which, although ostensibly psychological, would be genuinely spiritual. It could have been a peculiar expression of that fear and trembling which comes to a believer who is working out his own salvation in response to the activity of God in his life (Phil. 2:12-13). The locus of such activity would involve the subliminal level of personal life — the unknown or unconscious dimension — illustrated by what the letter to the Hebrews says of the Word of God as " living and active, sharper than any two-edged sword, piercing to the division of soul and spirit, of joints and marrow, and discerning the thoughts and intentions of the heart " (Heb. 4:12). With Paul, as with the letter to the Hebrews, it is the Word which, inseparably from the Spirit, searches the center of a man's life in such a manner. Thus, when we speak of the action of the one it is at the same time the action of the other. The ecstasy of tongues as the cathartic effect of such action would mean the creation of agape and thus a form of knowing, however incoherent its initial expression. It would still be characteristic of the babe in Christ, but at the point where the signs of spiritual infancy are pointing to spiritual maturity. For the mature believer, however, tongues would have little, if any, place. As one whose maturity derives from the fact that he has heard the gospel as revelation, his concern would be less for his edification than for his witness to others.

It is evident that Paul expected tongues to be interpreted, since he keeps returning to the theme from the beginning to the end of the chapter (I Cor. 14:5, 6, 13, 27-28). Although the tongues are incoherent, the important consideration is whether they are implicitly intelligible. This amounts to another criterion of acceptance along with agape, or more correctly, an expression of it. The meaning of intelligibility is not indicated, but since it is such that it edifies the church, it is related in some manner to the Word of God working within the ecstatic person. Without this, the ecstasy would be false.

Such a conception of the validity of tongues is consistent with Paul's preference for prophecy as a more desirable gift of the Spirit because of its intelligibility. " He who prophesies speaks to men for their upbuilding and encouragement and consolation." (V. 3.) Since all forms of worship should contribute to the edification of the church (v. 26), prophecy is especially desirable because it is devoted to this purpose. It is not a private religious exercise intended exclusively for the edification of the individual, but one concerned with the whole life of the church. As intelligible communication, it is evidence of a community consciousness which, in its capability of edifying the people of God, is an expression of agape. Vague, irrelevant communication of any kind in the church is an indication that the preacher does not love his people. Either he is concerned only for his private, mystical life and has no necessity laid upon him to communicate the gospel, or he is concerned only for his material interests, and feels no obligation to work on his subject matter and to communicate in the most relevant language possible. This suggests why Paul was compelled to say that in the church he would rather speak five words with his mind, in order to instruct others, than ten thousand words in a tongue (v. 19). It was not a question of the intelligible as an end in itself, but of evangelical responsibility grounded in agape.

Such a preference for the intelligible as we have it in prophecy — which for practical purposes means relevant preaching — should be considered in the light of the Jewish conception of the Spirit as the Spirit of prophecy. This conception associates the manifestation of the Spirit exclusively with the Word of God, which in late Judaism is particularly qualified by the understanding of Torah. Paul's insistence upon prophecy as a highly preferential gift seems in line with this conception. Although some contend that, strictly speaking, Paul reckons all miraculous phenomena among the manifestations of the Spirit, not recognizing the Jewish limitation to the Spirit of prophecy, this is not the case if we consider his evangelical reinterpretation of the Jewish conception. For whereas the Jewish conception restricts the manifestation of the Spirit to prophecy, Paul restricts it to Jesus Christ even when he speaks of a plurality of gifts from the same Spirit. This derives from the fact that for Paul the gift most typical of the Spirit as such is the confession that Jesus is Lord (ch. 12:3). The fact that all other gifts derive their true significance only through the manifestation of agape is only another way of saying that they derive it through this same Lord. In short, prophecy is evangelically defined by the confession. The fact, moreover, that for Paul the Spirit is " the power which involves him in the saving act of God through Christ " [61] should be understood as a further indication of the nature of the limitation. What we see in Paul's preference for prophecy, therefore, is a more thoroughly evangelical interpretation of the Jewish conception of the Spirit as the Spirit of prophecy than is commonly realized. This, as we have indicated, seems to have characterized his conception of tongues. The only ecstasy he could recognize was one that might be described as an ecstasy of the Word — an ecstasy implicitly intelligible and therefore capable of such interpretation as would edify the church.

This was not unrelated to the current of ecstasy in the history of Israel, which in some periods was more pronounced than in others but was always a component of the religious tradition. From earlier nabism, through classical prophetism, to later Judaism and the primitive church, whatever the form of the ecstasy, it seems always to have been qualified by the uniqueness of the faith of Israel and of the church, so that it was not the same ecstasy as in other religions and cultures. The difference may be illustrated in nabism, where, as Eichrodt indicates, there was a " ' concentration-ecstasy ' " as opposed to a " 'fusion-ecstasy,' " the latter typical of mysticism. The former was characterized by an awareness of the fundamental difference between God and man, so that instead of fusion it was an ecstasy in which the divine self-disclosure always confronted the prophet as something objective. The prophet himself was never assimilated into it.[62] In classical prophetism this was succeeded by a less ecstatic and a more personal understanding of the objectivity, so that the preeminence of the Word characterized the disclosure. A unique association between Word and Spirit seems to have obtained. When a similar association between prophecy and Spirit appears in late Judaism, and in Paul and the primitive church in a Christological form, it comes as no surprise. The Spirit of God signifies an ultimate intelligibility. On this basis, forms of ecstasy wholly physical or psychological in origin, or representative of mystical fusion and therefore not essentially intelligible, would be invalidated.

It is evident that Paul does not permit the worshiper to retire into the privacy of his subjective life or to lose himself in the mystery of the noumenal and to think that these are the highest forms of spirituality particularly when they are qualified by ecstasy. Since the Spirit is inseparable from the Word, the Spirit is inseparable from the intelligibility of the gospel of Christ, which is a scandal to the Jew and foolishness to the Gentile just because of its intelligibility. An ecstatic excursion into tongues, in which the intelligibility of the gospel is eclipsed in the experience of the worshiper, is an escape from the gospel. It is the same with vague, irrelevant, ill-prepared preaching, which, though not the equivalent of ecstatic tongues, is just as unintelligible. It is an escape into an unknown tongue. It is a disparagement of human language which is at the same time a disparagement of the Word of God.

How this happens in the modern situation and contributes to the irrelevance of preaching is sufficiently clear. " Exposed to the incessant and inexorably loquacious onslaught of the mass media, the press, and advertising, the man in the street becomes more and more skeptical of the language he is exposed to. The citizens of totalitarian countries know full well that most of what they are told is double-talk, devoid of real meaning. In the West, euphemisms and circumlocutions fill the press or resound from the pulpits. And advertising, by its constant use of superlatives, has succeeded in devaluating language to a point where it is a generally accepted axiom that most of the words one sees displayed on billboards or in the colored pages of magazine advertising are as meaningless as the jingles of television commercials. A yawning gulf has opened between language and reality." [63]

This quotation describes, in its own way, the problem of Paul in Corinth. It was the meaningless language of the religious world, rather than of the secular world, that was divorced from reality. The reality was the crucified Christ, to which relevant preaching testified. If all were to speak in tongues, who would hear the gospel or care to communicate it, or be edified by its interpretation? If all were to speak in tongues, what would happen to the preaching and teaching ministries? Would those who spoke in tongues contend that their ecstatic experience was of the essence of the gospel and that the absurdity of their utterances was identical with its offense?

We do not know to what extent speaking in ecstatic tongues was an attempt to rise above intelligible language and leave it behind as a sign of the flesh from which the human spirit would be free. Such a possibility would mean a certain contempt for language, which apart from complete silence could be very well expressed in absurd, irresponsible speech. This would be consistent with the fact that the phenomenon of ecstatic tongues in religion is not unrelated to those forms of modern art, music, and drama which are also unintelligible expressions of subjectivity. The incoherence of the tongues is no different in principle from the incoherence of the latter, particularly in what impresses the observer as a certain quality of madness. Each is an expression of what is inwardly significant to the individual as a function of pure freedom and as a disparagement of the representative, which, in language as in the arts, includes conventionality of meaning. It is the representative that is profoundly doubted in the modern skepticism of language and of the arts and that inevitably results in a retreat from the conceptual. The possibility of the conceptual's communicating the eternal, the human word the divine word, is called into question. The representative function of Biblical truths, doctrines, and belief is similarly denied. The only reality that remains is a pure freedom of the human spirit unhampered by logic, obligation, or conventionality of meaning in which even the identity of the self is doubted as another form of the conceptual not representative of a corresponding reality. The only language that remains is idle conversation, which, if transformed by loneliness into a compulsive need to talk, assumes an ecstatic quality not unlike that of speaking in tongues. "In a world that has lost its meaning, language also becomes a meaningless buzzing." Men have been "spattered with words that went dead as soon as they sounded; each word obliterated, before it had time to make sense, by the word that came next; so that in the end [they] did not know what had been said." [64]

The question that emerges from these observations is one that concerns the nature of language in relation to revelation. In the preaching of the gospel the human language is essentially the language of witness, and therefore only points, or testifies, to revelation. It is not conceptual language in the sense that concepts are assumed to enclose the truth of revelation as units and to communicate it directly to the hearer. The gospel language as a language of witness is a protest against the presumption of the conceptual in this alleged capacity, just as the pure freedom of those who abandon all intelligible language is a protest against it. This at once introduces the same distinctions employed in previous discussions of irresponsible freedom. Conceptualism here corresponds to the asceticism of the earlier chapters and leads to the bondage of literalism. As such it is the denial of the freedom of the Spirit (cf. II Cor. 3:6). But the answer is not to be found in the pure freedom of ecstatic tongues, which would abandon language and therefore dispense with all literalism in the manner of the libertines, who thought that all things were lawful for the believer. It is found in freedom limited in the interest of freedom, which seems implied in Paul's concern to permit tongues but to limit them by the discipline of agape. But since agape is essentially Christ the Living Word, it is this Word which limits the human word in the interest of its humanity. The problem of the nature of language is therefore a theological problem. The crisis of language is the crisis of faith, which is at the same time the crisis of love. All language and artistry are at best demonstrative, thus answering to the language of the gospel as witness. They only point; they never truly describe or explain, and when absolutized in such capacities they become idolatrous, with the result that the opposite idolatry is invoked as a reaction against them — an irresponsible linguistic libertinism in which men subordinate the conceptual.

XVIII

RESURRECTION AND IMMORTALITY
15:1-19

15 *Now I would remind you, brethren, in what terms I preached to you the gospel, which you received, in which you stand,* ² *by which you are saved, if you hold it fast — unless you believed in vain.*

3 *For I delivered to you as of first importance what I also received, that Christ died for our sins in accordance with the scriptures,* ⁴ *that he was buried, that he was raised on the third day in accordance with the scriptures,* ⁵ *and that he appeared to Cephas, then to the twelve.* ⁶ *Then he appeared to more than five hundred brethren at one time, most of whom are still alive, though some have fallen asleep.* ⁷ *Then he appeared to James, then to all the apostles.* ⁸ *Last of all, as to one untimely born, he appeared also to me.* ⁹ *For I am the least of the apostles, unfit to be called an apostle, because I persecuted the church of God.* ¹⁰ *But by the grace of God I am what I am, and his grace toward me was not in vain. On the contrary, I worked harder than any of them, though it was not I, but the grace of God which is with me.* ¹¹ *Whether then it was I or they, so we preach and so you believed.*

12 *Now if Christ is preached as raised from the dead, how can some of you say that there is no resurrection of the dead?* ¹³ *But if there is no resurrection of the dead, then Christ has not been raised;* ¹⁴ *if Christ has not been raised, then our preaching is in vain and your faith is in vain.* ¹⁵ *We are even found to be misrepresenting God, because we testified of God that he raised Christ, whom he did not raise if it is true that the dead are not raised.* ¹⁶ *For if the dead are not raised, then Christ has not been raised.* ¹⁷ *If Christ has not been raised, your faith is futile and you are still in your sins.*

*18 Then those also who have fallen asleep in Christ have perished.
19 If for this life only we have hoped in Christ, we are of all men
most to be pitied.*

The resurrection of the dead in its full, rich, and profound
significance may be regarded as the culmination of Paul's evangelical answer to the pastoral complexities of the Corinthian
church. It defines the perspective within which he views the
difficulties confronting him, just as it represents the heart of
the gospel he proclaims. This has been anticipated throughout
the letter not only in references to the Day of the Lord but in
the eschatological connotation that distinguishes the meaning
of salvation, maturity, responsible freedom, and agape. None
of these can be understood except in relation to the resurrection. The various problems throughout the letter have similarly
anticipated the resurrection, because for the most part they
have been essentially eschatological problems. For example,
the inclination of the Corinthians to absolutize the significant
persons in their lives in the form of idolatrous loyalties involved
the absolutizing of the present by the autonomy of their judgments. There was an eschatological error implicit in these loyalties, just as there is in the modern cult of personality
(ch. 4:3-5). The fascination of some of the Corinthians for
pure freedom involved an implicitly destructive component of
eschatological significance. Moreover, the extent to which
destruction, spiritual peril, and eschatological judgment thread
their way, as a complex theme, through the letter prepares us
for the final problem of death, for which the resurrection is
the answer. Since at each stage the ultimate predicament in its
human, divine, and demonic dimensions has been confronting
us, we are prepared for Paul's elaboration upon it at the end.
The fifteenth chapter is therefore not a chapter which merely
adds another problem to an extended list. Rather, it comprehends all the previous problems, just as it comprehends all the
previous answers.

Like all considerations of destiny, the peculiar error of the

Corinthians undoubtedly influenced their outlook on life and qualified the manner in which they were motivated in practical affairs. What men think of their ultimate end is not unrelated to the goals for which they strive nor to their conception of the success of their labors. If they feel they are caught or trapped by the enormity of economic or political systems, so that there is no way out, if their existence seems only a futile struggle in which the strong and the cunning triumph, their motivational pattern will be profoundly affected. A retreat into subjectivity or the exploitation of momentary pleasures will be the probable reaction to the predicament. The inclination to live in the immediacy of the present will conceal the unacknowledged doubt of what there is to come. Those whose years are declining may prefer to retreat into the memories of the past or to fan the fires of youth. None will " press on toward the goal for the prize of the upward call of God in Christ Jesus " (Phil. 3:14).

The particular error that prompted Paul to elaborate the doctrine of the resurrection of the dead is not precisely identified. As an error that may be generally described as an inability to believe that the resurrection is integral to the gospel, it was a perversion of such proportions that it called the gospel into question along with the pastoral directives based upon it. Paul's sensitivity to this fact probably explains why he reminds the Corinthians at the opening of the chapter of the essential content of the gospel, by which they are saved if they believe (ch. 15:1-4). Here the death and resurrection of Christ are the two indispensable and interrelated events with which the gospel is mainly concerned. The fact that he presents them together and immediately expands on the historical attestation of the resurrection of Christ is an indication of the kind of error which confronted him. "For I delivered to you as of first importance what I also received, that Christ died for our sins in accordance with the scriptures, that he was buried, that he was raised on the third day in accordance with the scriptures" (vs. 3-4). To use a geometrical illustration, the gospel is like an ellipse with its two foci — the one the death of Christ, the other the resurrection. To eliminate either focus would eliminate the whole ellipse. Indeed, this double focus seems to determine the theological structure of the letter, with the one elaborated in the first chapter and the other in the fifteenth chapter, and the intervening consideration of problems and answers influenced by it.

It is the intention of Paul to leave no doubt that the death and resurrection of Christ are both in accordance with the Scriptures. His emphasis suggests that the death and resurrection are no merely novel or extraneous possibilities that might have been in accordance with other traditions as familiar to the Corinthians as the traditions of the mystery cults. Instead, they fulfill the deepest expectations of the Scriptural norms of the covenanted community. If the omission of references should cast doubt on this claim, or the Old Testament Scriptures themselves seem not to justify it, at least the confidences to which they testify would make some rather basic anticipations of the death and resurrection of Christ inevitable. For since these Scriptures recognize that God is the creator of the visible world and of the human body, that he is the Lord of life and death, whose merciful action is on behalf of the whole man, that he is the gracious one whose covenantal relationship with his people involves a unique concern for the poor, humble, and broken — and this with Messianic expectations and a deep awareness of the guilt and mortality of man — then it is not accidental that there should be some foreshadowing of what was to come in Christ. On this point Barth makes a significant observation:

"Paul knows he is in harmony with the 'scriptures' when on the grounds of revelation he testifies that Christ died for our sins and rose the third day. He sees the fathers of the Old Testament all standing . . . around this turning point from death to life, . . . all expecting, believing, and promising in many different tongues nothing else but this one. . . . All of them with all the historical obscurity which lies over their personalities and thoughts are intelligible from this point of view. It cannot be a question of details." [65]

In vs. 5-8, Paul submits historical evidence of the resurrection of Christ which has particular reference to those who witnessed his appearances: " He appeared to Cephas, then to the twelve. Then he appeared to more than five hundred brethren at one time, most of whom are still alive, though some have fallen asleep. Then he appeared to James, then to all the apostles. Last of all, as to one untimely born, he appeared also to me." The ostensible purpose of such evidence is to emphasize the historicity of the resurrection. Since the bodily resurrection of believers is the issue on which the argument of the chapter turns, we can scarcely avoid the conclusion that Paul understands the appearances to be bodily in nature. Although his pneumatic conception of the risen body (vs. 42-50) would qualify the conclusion, it is nevertheless a question of the personal confrontation of Christ in a peculiarly objective manner and not simply a vision. Such testimony obviously closes the door against any tendency to regard the resurrection as mythical, as if its only significance were that of an incident in a mythological drama. Consequently, it would be totally contrary to Paul's historical understanding of the event to consider it as merely the religious personification of natural vitality which awakens in the spring because it was only dormant during the winter and never dead. By the same token it would be equally contrary to his understanding of the event to regard it as an esoteric representation of the psychological emergence of the real self following the death of the pseudo self in the process of individuation. With him it is not a question of mythology or psychology but history.

In this respect, however, the offense of the cross is repeated in the resurrection. The scandal and the foolishness of the one (ch. 1:23) is manifested in the other. Instead of Christ's being so different from men's thoughts of him that he appeared to be a criminal and was executed, he is so different that not even death could destroy him; his emergence from the grave defies the natural and the empirical. To the secular man, this is wholly absurd, and the thought of it a childish legend or superstition intolerable in a scientific age. It angers him more than the offense of the criminal Christ because he can possibly assimilate the latter as a revolutionary, but not the former, whose victory over death is contrary to all he knows. Yet he seldom expresses himself so strongly when with less disturbance to himself he can achieve as much by total indifference. What specifically offends him, just as it offended some in the ancient Corinthian church, is the possibility of the resurrection of the body. Whether the resurrection, for all its strangeness, is less surprisingly incredible than the mystery of death, and whether the strangeness of the answer is not appropriate to the strangeness of the problem, is not considered.

The difficulty in understanding why Paul submitted testimony to the resurrection, however, is that he provides little or no precise information on the error it was intended to correct. Ostensibly, it emphasized the historicity of the resurrection. But the trend of verses twelve to nineteen implies that the Corinthians had not doubted that Christ had risen from the dead; they had only doubted the possibility of their own resurrection as a consequence of his. This follows from the argument that " if Christ is preached as raised from the dead, how can some of you say that there is no resurrection of the dead? But if there is no resurrection of the dead, then Christ has not been raised " (vs. 12-13). In a word, they cannot deny the one and yet hold to the other. They have to be consistent.

The evidence suggests that they thought of his resurrection in a class by itself and therefore appropriate to his uniqueness. Although they believed it to be historical, they seem to have reduced it to the status of an isolated event that had no relevance for them except perhaps as a demonstration of his deity. In what manner they conceived of it as a bodily resurrection is nowhere indicated. Perhaps it was comparable to an apocalyptic assumption, as with Moses and Elijah, who were believed to have been taken up into heaven bodily. Perhaps it was conceived in gnostic fashion, in which, strictly speaking, there was no resurrection but a return of the Redeemer to heaven, who in his escape from death was conceived as acting spiritually, with the historical character of the event greatly attenuated.

The manner in which they isolated the resurrection is suggested by Paul's comments in vs. 14, 17-18: " If Christ has not been raised, then our preaching is in vain and your faith is in vain. . . . You are still in your sins. Then those also who have fallen asleep in Christ have perished." This would indicate that however they may have conceived the resurrection of Christ as historical, they had isolated it from the total Christ-event. They had not considered it integral to the gospel. To be more specific, the event " was raised " (v. 4) had not been considered integral to the event that preceded it, i.e., " died for our sins " (v. 3), just as it had not been considered integral to the event that followed it, i.e., " appeared to " (vs. 5-8). The three events had not been recognized as one comprehensive event. In other words, their conception of the resurrection as an isolated event had not implied that the risen Christ would relate himself to these witnesses in what was essentially revelation.[66] It was resurrection independent not only of Christ's victory over sin but of revelation as that by which the believer participates in the benefits of the victory. It is true, of course, from Paul's description of himself as the last of those who witnessed the appearances, that the Corinthians could not be included among those he named. But they could have received the revelation by which they would have become spiritually mature (ch. 2:9-10). For they were not unlike the immature (the babes in Christ) who earlier in the letter had failed to understand the gospel for a similar reason. They had not heard it as revelation and therefore as the event-ful word of truth in their lives. Accordingly, we have to recognize that Paul's purpose in adducing the testimony to the resurrection of Christ was more than that of emphasizing its historicity. It was to indicate that the resurrection event was implicitly revelation. It was Christ relating himself to others in a manner creative of a fellowship of witnesses.

The source of the difficulty for the Corinthians was that they could not see the necessity of bodily resurrection as definitive of their salvation. Although we do not know their precise understanding of the Christian hope, it is highly probable that they subscribed to the doctrine of the immortality of the soul. The Platonic tradition and the contemporary gnostic tendencies were influential in disseminating the doctrine. The body was considered the tomb or prison house of the soul, from which the soul would be released at death. The soul was considered prior to the body, whereas the body, in contrast to the soul, was associated with sin and death. Indeed, some of Paul's language — such as his exclamatory cry, "Wretched man that I am! Who will deliver me from this body of death?" (Rom. 7:24) — may have been misunderstood at this point. Thus, to put the Corinthians' understanding of the doctrine of immortality into the commonest terms, it was enough to know that when they died they would go to heaven.

It will be evident that the Corinthian error was similar to much of the eschatological hope prevalent in contemporary Christianity. Belief in the resurrection of Christ is affirmed but largely restricted to the Easter season, and is not being adequately recognized at other times of the year as integral to the Christ-event and to the gospel. The cross is separated from the resurrection, as if the cross by itself constituted the gospel. Certain evangelical hymns reflect this one-sidedness. The familiar "Rock of Ages, Cleft for Me," for example, which in its rich concentration upon the cross warms the Christian heart, fails to speak of the resurrection in equally positive language and fades out into the generality of soaring through tracts unknown and of seeing God on his judgment throne. Indeed, in much evangelical Christianity this doctrine of immortality is attached to personal faith in Christ in a manner that suggests that his resurrection contains no promise of itself and at best is only a guarantee of immortality. This means that salvation pertains only to the soul and not to the whole man, as the doctrine of the resurrection of the body implies. The attitude toward the body is less negative than in Platonism, and much less negative than in gnosticism, with the concentration upon the soul often more of an escape from evangelical responsibility for the body than is commonly recognized.

Although it would be unwarranted to describe the Corinthian error as representative of a middle-class eschatology, this could be said with considerable truth of the doctrine of immortality in the modern church. The salvation of the soul easily becomes a doctrinal rationalization for keeping religion in its place, with its responsibility restricted to the individual and to the subjective, so that it is unable to speak relevantly into real life. The sovereignty of God tends to be limited to the next world, and within the present world, largely to the inward things of the soul, which are assumed to be private, and without political, economic, or social implications. Everything tends to be spiritualized so that it is forgotten that men have bodies to feed and clothe, through which they are involved objectively with others and with the world around them. Consequently the doctrine of immortality, which is individualistic, subjective, and mystical, presupposes a perspective inconsistent with that presupposed by the resurrection of the body. By the attachment of the doctrine of immortality to faith in Christ, the latter is profoundly altered. The cross is separated from the resurrection and set in the noneschatological context of generalized religious experience. Under these circumstances, even the resurrection of Christ tends to be regarded as only a special instance of immortality. Easter comes to mean only that his spirit returned to heaven.[67]

But why was the resurrection necessary? Why did Paul not only say, in Rom. 4:25, that Christ was put to death for our trespasses but that he was raised for our justification? The answer will begin to emerge as we realize how different the forgiveness of Christ is from the forgiveness one man may offer another. The forgiveness of the latter is for the most part an overlooking of wrong rather than an undoing of wrong, more subjective rather than a basic restitution of a broken relationship. It is obviously not the rectification of objective guilt. But more particularly, it is the way in which the resurrection of Christ makes his forgiveness count that defines the difference. For if Christ had died and remained dead, his forgiveness would have died with him. It would not have been available to men as it is from him as the risen Christ. The underlying reason for this will be understood by the interrelation of the power of sin with the power of death. In some mysterious way the two are manifestations of the same power. This can be partially appreciated from the fact that in ordinary life sin has an inexorable tendency of leading to death, of which war is the most extreme example. It is literally true that the wages of sin is death. Thus, in any deep and effective sense there can be no victory over the one that is not at the same time a victory over the other. The failure to see this probably derives from the prevalent tendency to regard sin as a moral, rather than as an eschatological, category.

But why is the body of Christ necessary for such a dual victory? Why would the victory not have been as deep and effective if his spirit had died and risen again without the body? What has the body to do with the victory over sin and death? To appreciate the answer it is important to remember that the body is the symbol of his identification with the humanity of man and his organic relation with the historical process. The declaration that the Word became flesh is equivalent in meaning to the sinful connotation of " flesh " qualifying the human and the historical. It is because sin and death pertain not merely to the private and the subjective but to the whole of existence in its human and historical dimension that Christ lived a bodily life, suffered in his body, and was raised in his body. The Biblical emphasis on his body signifies the action of the whole Christ as a particular expression of the love of the Creator for the creatureliness of the man and the world He has made.

These observations prepare the way for an understanding of why the bodily resurrection of the believer is a necessary aspect of the Christian interpretation of destiny. Expressed somewhat generally, it is the ultimate objectification of the agape of God comprehensive of the whole man and of the order of existence in which he lives. The agape of God in its ultimate manifestation does not pertain exclusively to an inner core, soul, spirit, or real self that is allegedly immune from the power of sin and death and that has a supposed affinity to divinity, or a continuity or identity with deity that suggests at this point no essential need of such redemptive agape. It pertains to the whole man — to the wholeness of his personal existence, to the social and cosmic order in which his personal existence finds expression and meaning and which is part of him and he part of it. It derives from the fact that the Bible takes the body and the historical and cosmic order seriously because of their origin in the gracious act of the Creator. It therefore forbids the practice of putting them on a lower plane than the spiritual defined merely as their opposites. In this respect the doctrine of the resurrection of the body possesses a wholesome secular connotation in contrast to the doctrine of the immortality of the soul, with its religious connotation.

It implies a radical doctrine of sin and death that applies to the whole man both individually and collectively. The body as a symbol of his organic relation to the historical order is indicative of the fact that the sin and death of the individual is correlative with the corruption of the social order. But this corruption is of such magnitude that neither law nor revolution do more than effect certain relative improvements that fail to eradicate the source of the trouble. For the injustice derives from the cosmic order. It derives not only from the individual and society but from nature, as any man discovers who is mysteriously dehumanized by nature when it is absolutized. For nature is " red in tooth and claw " with blood, as the prophet seemed to understand in the formulation of his ultimate hope that the wolf would dwell with the lamb, and the leopard lie down with the kid, and the calf and the lion together, and a little child would lead them (Isa. 11:6). Or, as it has been rightly discerned, " we hang men for what nature does everyday " (J. S. Mill). Thus, if there is to be any ultimate answer to the mysteriously interrelated problem of sin and death, it must be individual, social, and cosmic in its dimensions, as the doctrine of the resurrection signifies. It must involve the transformation represented by the eschatological end as Paul conceives it. In this transformation the resurrection may be considered as the fulfillment at the end of the promise implicit in creation at the beginning.

XIX

THE NATURE AND CONQUEST
OF DEATH

15:20-34

15 *But in fact Christ has been raised from the dead, the first fruits of those who have fallen asleep.* ²¹ *For as by a man came death, by a man has come also the resurrection of the dead.* ²² *For as in Adam all die, so also in Christ shall all be made alive.* ²³ *But each in his own order: Christ the first fruits, then at his coming those who belong to Christ.* ²⁴ *Then comes the end, when he delivers the kingdom to God the Father after destroying every rule and every authority and power.* ²⁵ *For he must reign until he has put all his enemies under his feet.* ²⁶ *The last enemy to be destroyed is death.* ²⁷ *"For God has put all things in subjection under his feet." But when it says, " All things are put in subjection under him," it is plain that he is expected who put all things under him.* ²⁸ *When all things are subjected to him, then the Son himself will also be subjected to him who put all things under him, that God may be everything to every one.*

²⁹ *Otherwise, what do people mean by being baptized on behalf of the dead? If the dead are not raised at all, why are people baptized on their behalf?* ³⁰ *Why am I in peril every hour?* ³¹ *I protest, brethren, by my pride in you which I have in Christ Jesus our Lord, I die every day!* ³² *What do I gain if, humanly speaking, I fought with beasts at Ephesus? If the dead are not raised, " Let us eat and drink, for tomorrow we die."* ³³ *Do not be deceived: " Bad company ruins good morals."* ³⁴ *Come to your right mind, and sin no more. For some have no knowledge of God. I say this to your shame.*

The problem of death has been anticipated in the seriousness of Paul's concern to save men from perishing, which has
colored everything he has previously said in the letter. It has
undoubtedly qualified his sensitivity to the possibility of destruction as this possibility has arisen out of the various expressions of irresponsible freedom. Rivalry and strife, sexual
and religious extremities of conduct as manifestations of eros,
all have an inward affinity to death, and in their lawlessness
contribute to it. In a world whose form is passing away (ch.
7:31) these are but the symptoms of the sickness unto death
from which it suffers. It cannot be said, therefore, that in
speaking of death in the fifteenth chapter Paul is suddenly
introducing a new subject, but only that he is speaking more
explicitly of what has been on his mind all along.

In keeping with the trend of Biblical thought on the subject, Paul's conception of death is not that of a natural biological process accepted as part of life but that of an inimical
power that is foreign to the original purpose of the created
order. As the last enemy that will be destroyed in the eschatological end (ch. 15:26), it is evidently conceived by Paul as
an evil, angelic power, according to his allusion in v. 24 to
what are evidently various orders of angelic beings (cf. Rom.
8:38). The destruction of death, as the last of the forms of
opposition to God, is necessary for the establishment of his
Kingdom.

How it acquired such dominion over the created order is
explained by the fall of Adam, who, as the representative of
sinful, mortal humanity, acted for all men corporately. " By
a man came death " is the simple way Paul puts it, just as he
puts the allusion to its corporateness: " In Adam all die "
(I Cor. 15:21-22). The same explanation is given at greater
length in Romans, where it is said that as sin came into the
world through one man and death through sin, so death spread
to all men because all have sinned (Rom. 5:12). Later in the
same letter, death is regarded as having spread to the whole
natural world in its subjection to futility and to the bondage
of decay (ch. 8:20-21).

Such a conception of the origin and nature of death, which will strike the modern mind as strange and prescientific, can be best appreciated by the way it calls attention to the fact that death is more than a biological problem. The emphasis is on the human and personal aspects of death, which qualify it as a problem of man in his consciousness of himself as more than an animal and more than a product of nature. As an enemy of man, death is not only a terminal event in his life but a condition which at every stage qualifies his life as a struggle for existence — a struggle against death as the inexorable threat to his security. The fact that he has to live with the threat means that he is less conscious of it except in critical situations. But this does not mean that at the unconscious level he is not responsive to it as a basic source of anxiety. It is a threat that makes the preservation of his organic integrity the first law of his being, and his responsiveness to it is implicit in the unconscious maintenance of his organic unity.

The inimical character of death is associated with the indifference of nature to the human and personal interests of man. It represents the cold, inanimate state to which he as a human being and as a person inevitably returns. It is that state to which the familiar text refers: " You are dust, and to dust you shall return " (Gen. 3:19). In spite of the fact that man is able to wrest from nature many benefits, he cannot escape recognizing its inanimate character as the objectification of death. Even the knowledge he obtains from nature partakes of this objectivity in its cold, scientific character, which for this reason requires him to die to himself in the inward achievement of objectivity. In this sense he dies in the interest of dead truth and is depersonalized in spirit long before he becomes aware of it in his outward life. All natural life is relatively unstable and repeatedly returns to the inanimate state in a ruthless succession of generations, regardless of the species. Nature in this respect is as indifferent to the human species as to the individual. The whole of humanity could disappear as readily as some prehistoric species without nature's manifesting the slightest ripple of concern. If men have "read" their animism into nature, it is still theirs, so that the mystical absorption into nature is but the absorption into death — a surrender not only of the personal but of all that is characteristically human in the return to the inanimate state. If they have sought this in religion, why is it felt to be inconsistent that the nuclear extermination of the human race as a blitzlike consummation of such a spiritual objective should be so terrible?

In Paul's interpretation of the origin of death, man is held responsible. For it is a condition which, as a consequence of his guilt, is representative of the judgment of God. If this is difficult to understand, particularly in its significance for the whole of nature, at least it can be recognized that for Paul, as for Biblical thought generally, the problem of death is implicitly the problem of guilt. It is therefore not adequately described as the threat of nonbeing. Death is not a reversion to nonbeing in the sense of nothingness but a symbol of separation from God and one's people, and in its ultimate form, equivalent to hell. It is essentially the separation that derives from guilt. If Paul sees this as relevant to the whole of nature in its bondage to death, it is probably because he views nature within the context of history, rather than history within the context of nature. If so, his conception of such bondage is suggestive of an original form of guilt. The reason for such a conception of death is that the reality of God, for him as for Biblical faith, was greater than the reality of the world ("being") or of death as secularly conceived ("nonbeing"). The reality of the transcendent God made it evident that the difference between the world ("being") and death ("nonbeing") is only a relative difference — not the absolute difference it is for the modern secular man. This man, as an atheist, has absolutized the present world so that with it he has absolutized death as "nonbeing." The problem for him is no longer separation and guilt but annihilation and meaninglessness. Even when he is not avowedly atheistic, his total involvement in immediacy, encouraged by his fascination for the present world, makes him inherently atheistic.

For Paul, as for Biblical faith generally, the reality of God is manifest in the call of God, which is creative of a covenanted community and of the individuality of its members. In this way both the community and its members have a particularity tantamount to a unique and radical personalism. Both have an awareness that the call of God as a manifestation of his mercy gives to them and to their history a purpose that preserves them from the temptation of regarding themselves merely as biological accidents of a blind natural process. As those who are called, they are aware of themselves not as victims of a blind fate but as free men whose freedom is always of the quality indicated by the text, " If God is for us, who is against us? " But it is the personal quality of what binds them to God and to one another, which is best characterized as agape, that makes death such a problem for them, although not the final problem. For he who loves profoundly and with integrity will always suffer when death intervenes to disrupt the relationship. In this respect, agape and death are mutually exclusive. If the one is the answer to the problem of destiny, the other cannot be.

This, however, is not the opposition to death that is derived from a selfish desire to live and from the will to power and that always reacts to the threat of death with a comparable form of fear or anger. Indeed, the opposition to death derived from pure freedom — a lawless, loveless defiance of the threat of nonbeing — can never be minimized as a characteristic of man. From this point of view, death can very well be regarded as an enemy. Nor is there any essential difference between such defiance and its ascetic, negative phase, which, instead of standing in opposition to death, advocates resignation to it. Instead of escaping from death, it escapes into it. Instead of a wordliness that absolutizes the world (" being ") as its equivalent of God, it is a religion that absolutizes death (" nonbeing ") as its equivalent of God. The subtlety of its appeal is probably greater than we believe if we allow the contention " that all men, unconsciously it may be, nourish in their hearts a secret desire for nothingness, a desire to have done

with the storm-swept world in which they feel themselves
strangers and aliens, and to be at home in the only perfect
country in the wide universe, the land of dreamless sleep, . . .
that the thoughts of peace, eternity, God, are merely a veiled
longing for death, the consoling vision of the fugitives from
existence, the familiar preference of the mystics for the perfection of eternity to the known perfections of time — ' rejoicing secretly in the divine perfections of the grave.' " [68]

But neither such resignation as a form of asceticism nor the
defiance of death as a form of libertinism, which are but positive and negative phases of pure freedom, have anything to
do with agape as the answer to the problem of human destiny.
If the one is commonly regarded as religious and the other as
secular, the difference is negligible in comparison to their essential unity. Both find their common origin in the spirit of
man, in the conviction that God cannot be other than some
equivalent of " being " (world-nature) or of "nonbeing "
(death-nothingness). Both are essentially loveless and therefore not bound to God or to man according to the Biblical
conception of the convenantal relationship. Consequently,
they are expressions of irresponsibility in which the problem
of guilt is not recognized as integral to the problem of death.

But since no one ever escapes responsibility, either in his
defiance of death or in his resignation to it, the problem of
guilt is never wholly evaded. It seems to arise from an awareness of the destructive within us and within the world with
which we are identified and from a corresponding awareness
of our responsibility for it. If this has been traditionally understood as sin, it is probably understood more relevantly in
the modern world as the mysterious source of such destructiveness. This guilt of sin is strangely compounded of death
in contributing to the destructive potentiality of modern society, which is at once political, economic, and psychological,
and as Paul would add, eschatological. The threat of the nuclear extermination of the human race is the symbol of a destructiveness that has its counterpart in the psychical structur-
ing and conditioning of the modern man by all the varying

social and economic circumstances in which he lives. The outward threat is only a sign of the inward threat and an indication of the deep spiritual crisis represented by the cheapening of life in the modern world. As a destructiveness that testifies to the ultimate meaning of death, it shows that death is not adequately defined in biological terms. There is no biological precedent for such destructiveness, nothing comparable to it in the animal world, especially in the strange correlation it has with the intelligence of man, with the freedom of science and the prodigious expansion of knowledge. In its unprecedented proportions it has acquired apocalyptic significance in relation to modern history, and in secular form has confronted us with ultimate questions for which there are only eschatological answers.

Returning now to the error of the Corinthians for which Paul's interpretation of the nature and conquest of death is a necessary corrective, it can be said that they failed to recognize the scope of the redemptive purpose of God in Christ. Just as popular conceptions of God are often too small, the Corinthian conception of his redemptive purpose was too small. " They had comprehended what had happened in Christ in the world as something finished and satisfying in itself." [69] They had not recognized that it was only the beginning of an achievement that was to embrace their whole being and the whole natural order of existence. They had not recognized that it was only the first victory in a conflict that was to end in the overthrow of all that was in opposition to God in the social and cosmic order, and in the establishment of his Kingdom over all.

The appraisal of their error as a form of perfectionism, which probably meant that they thought themselves saved instead of being saved (I Cor. 1:18: *tois sōzomenois hēmin;* cf. Rom. 8.23), will be clarified by these observations of Barth: " The Christian monism of the Corinthians who regarded the Kingdom of God as already established is pious godlessness. . . . As Christ himself allows his enemies no peace, so for Christians there can be no security of an alleged possession in the shadow of the coming. . . . The aim of the movement which is the meaning of the Kingdom of Christ, is the abolition of death [I Cor. 15:26]. Death is the peak of all that is contrary to God in the world, the last enemy, thus not the natural lot of man, not an unalterable divine dispensation. . . . Peace cannot and must not be concluded just here in such a way as to establish a spiritual-religious-moral Kingdom of God on earth, while forgetting the enemy." [70]

The manner in which Paul represents this victory, upon the return of Christ, under the form of a final conflict with dark, demonic powers, epitomized by death and the resultant establishment of the Kingdom of God, bears a significance that may not be apparent from the apocalyptic imagery. The well-known difficulties of interpreting the order of events (I Cor. 15:23-28) detailed by Paul only to the extent of providing assurance to the Corinthians should not obscure the nature of the hope he set before them.[71] This involves an extreme tension between the present situation, in which the main problem of humanity is that of objective guilt, death, and the dark riddle of nature and the future situation in which these will be overcome. The realism of such hope, which would see in these the kind of predicament not overcome by moral achievement, by psychical or mystical insight, or by scientific or revolutionary action, is not essentially pessimistic. It is qualified by the recognition that the natural and cosmic order was created by God. It represents a profound loyalty to the whole of this order, as it does to the whole man collectively and individually. The presupposition of the hope Paul set before the Corinthians is the fulfillment of the original purpose of creation, which is now obscured by dark and evil powers. Such fulfillment in the eschatological end is not a static end in which everything comes to a standstill but a new order, a new freedom that enables creation to issue in all its rich variety of potentiality. In this respect it is the revelation of the glory of God. This is the thought implicit in the optimism of Paul when he says that " the sufferings of this present time are not worth comparing with the glory that is to be revealed to us. For the creation waits with eager longing for the revealing of the sons of God; . . . because the creation itself will be set free from its bondage to decay and obtain the glorious liberty of the children of God " (Rom. 8:18-19, 21).

In such hope we have the culmination of the radical personalism of the Bible as the answer to the problem of destiny. The ultimate is not merely mind or intelligence or the personal as they are commonly conceived in the context of guilt, death, and darkness, but as they are revealed in Christ, whose redemptive action is the agape of God. As the mediator of the agape of God, he is not an independent God, as the Corinthian Christ cult might have presumed, but one who in the end subjects himself to the Father and thereby testifies to the fact that the will of the one is in harmony with the will of the other. As such it is consistent with Paul's assertion in the second letter that God was in Christ reconciling the world to himself. His agape, which is comprehensive of his mind and intelligence, and definitive of the personal, is representative of the secret of existence and its fulfillment. In this respect it is representative of the secret of the resurrection as the fulfillment of creation. The same radical personalism is descriptive of the role that it is possible for man to have in such fulfillment through faith in Christ. This is not fantasy or a religious form of escape from the realities of the present but an optimism which, while loyal to the whole man and to the whole social and cosmic order as created of God, is ruthlessly honest in its understanding of their fundamental predicament. If it is a sign of man's alienation from himself and from nature, it concerns only the alienation defined by guilt and death and the nihilism of nature. It is not the kind of otherwordliness which is little more than an abandonment of responsibility for the present world, but the opposite. The same paradoxical relationship between such hope and a concern for the present obtains, according to which the hope confers a profound meaningfulness upon everything that is done in the present. If it prevents the absolutizing of the present as illustrated by idolatrous attachments to personality, money and property, and institutions such as the church and state, this should not obscure the fact that it is creative of a genuine love and responsibility for others.

The effect of such a hope upon the motivation of Christian conduct, as illustrated by Paul's appeal to the obscure practice of baptism for the dead and to his fighting with beasts at Ephesus, confirms this observation. Baptism of any kind, if we may be guided by his interpretation of its essential meaning in the sixth chapter of Romans (vs. 1-4), is a participation in the death and resurrection of Christ. What Paul is probably reminding them in the case of baptism for the dead is that baptism is not only such participation but a promise of their resurrection to come. In such action they are unwittingly testifying to such a hope — which should be understood by every believer and therefore effective in his conduct as that present reality which is determinative of his motivation.

Whether Paul fought with beasts at Ephesus or spoke in a figurative manner of enemies with beastlike propensities, his illustration is even more relevant to the nature of his motivation. If the dead are not raised, why should he incur such risk? If there is no hope which confers significance on his present conduct, so that it counts eternally, why should he not rather eat and drink and exploit the pleasurable possibilities of the present in the realization that tomorrow he will die? Why should he and his fellow apostles endure the stigma of the refuse of the world and the offscouring of all things if it is of no avail? Why should they exhibit agape toward others at such cost if it is of no lasting significance? Why not rather be selfish and as acquisitive as possible while the opportunity lasts? On this basis it is not difficult to see why, if in this life we who are in Christ have only hope, we are of all men most to be pitied (I Cor. 15:19). The sacrifice, the risk, and the agape that reaches out to others would then be all a measure of our madness.

What a man's conception of his death and destiny may be is therefore not a matter of indifference to present conduct. If he thinks he derives from nothingness and returns to nothingness, the inclination to assume that his life is another form of nothingness will be more difficult to resist. If such a persuasion seizes his generation and pervades the world in which he lives, the conviction of what some have called the infinite and everlasting value of the individual will quickly vanish. Life will become cheap. No qualms of conscience will afflict the agents of dehumanization. The purveyors of destruction will not hesitate in the procurement of megadeaths. For many the prospect of suicide will seem preferable to the pathos of a meaningless existence. For others the irresoluble alternative "to be or not to be" will tend to paralyze their action. But for most, the necessity of convincing themselves of their importance by pride, achievement, and power, and of persuading themselves that their lives and work count for a greater or lesser time, will be of primary concern. It all suggests that paralleling man's urge to preserve his organic integrity as the first law of his being is the urge to preserve his self-esteem. Failing this, the self tends to disintegrate in a manner comparable to the disintegration of the organism when the will to live declines. If this is true, it will illuminate the motivation of the modern status seekers and of those who long to be accepted and liked. Although various immediate circumstances explain this motivation, it is not exclusive of the deeper and subtler meaninglessness that conditions the practical motivation of great numbers of people. It will indicate that when, out of an awareness of what the hope of the resurrection meant to him, Paul warned the Corinthians of the moral effect of bad company (v. 33), his exhortation had other than an ordinary meaning. His urging that they come to their right mind and sin no more had reference to the avoidance of those who had no knowledge of God (v. 34) because they had no hope.

XX

RESURRECTION AND RESUSCITATION
15:35-58

15 *But some one will ask, " How are the dead raised? With what kind of body do they come? "* [36] *You foolish man! What you sow does not come to life unless it dies.* [37] *And what you sow is not the body which is to be, but a bare kernel, perhaps of wheat or of some other grain.* [38] *But God gives it a body as he has chosen, and to each kind of seed its own body.* [39] *For not all flesh is alike, but there is one kind for men, another for animals, another for birds, and another for fish.* [40] *There are celestial bodies and there are terrestrial bodies; but the glory of the celestial is one, and the glory of the terrestrial is another.* [41] *There is one glory of the sun, and another glory of the moon, and another glory of the stars; for star differs from star in glory.*

42 *So is it with the resurrection of the dead. What is sown is perishable, what is raised is imperishable.* [43] *It is sown in dishonor, it is raised in glory. It is sown in weakness, it is raised in power.* [44] *It is sown a physical body, it is raised a spiritual body. If there is a physical body, there is also a spiritual body.* [45] *Thus it is written, " The first man Adam became a living being "; the last Adam became a life-giving spirit.* [46] *But it is not the spiritual which is first but the physical, and then the spiritual.* [47] *The first man was from the earth, a man of dust; the second man is from heaven.* [48] *As was the man of dust, so are those who are of the dust; and as is the man of heaven, so are those who are of heaven.* [49] *Just as we have borne the image of the man of dust, we shall also bear the image of the man of heaven.* [50] *I tell you this, brethren: flesh and blood cannot inherit the kingdom of God, nor does the perishable inherit the imperishable.*

210

51 *Lo! I tell you a mystery. We shall not all sleep, but we shall all be changed,* [52] *in a moment, in the twinkling of an eye, at the last trumpet. For the trumpet will sound, and the dead will be raised imperishable, and we shall be changed.* [53] *For this perishable nature must put on the imperishable, and this mortal nature must put on immortality.* [54] *When the perishable puts on the imperishable, and the mortal puts on immortality, then shall come to pass the saying that is written:*

" Death is swallowed up in victory."
[55] *" O death, where is thy victory?*
O death, where is thy sting? "
[56] *The sting of death is sin, and the power of sin is the law.* [57] *But thanks be to God, who gives us the victory through our Lord Jesus Christ.*

58 *Therefore, my beloved brethren, be steadfast, immovable, always abounding in the work of the Lord, knowing that in the Lord your labor is not in vain.*

One of the barriers to the belief in the resurrection of the body is its inconceivability. The mortality of man and the nature of death as a biological process make it seem absurd and therefore qualified by the same offense that was evident in the cross as a scandal to the Jews and folly to the Gentiles. In one form or another the question always arises: " How are the dead raised? With what kind of body do they come? " (v. 35). Typical of the rationalist in every man, it is a question that might have been put in other ways: Will the body be that of childhood, youth, or age? Will it be the healthy body of the best years or the sickly or afflicted body of the worst years? Or, if not a literal inquiry into the identity of the body the same rationalism may be concerned with more abstruse matters: How will the dead be fed if raised? How will living space be found in an overpopulated world? Or the more complex question of the ancient Sadducees may be posed: Whose wife in the resurrection will a woman be who is successively widowed of seven husbands (Luke 20:27-33)? Speculation of this type was not uncommon in the first century, particularly in reaction to the doctrine of the resurrection as one of the tenets of Pharisaism. Almost the same question that some of the Corinthians put to Paul appears in the Apocalypse of Baruch (ch. 49:1): "In what shape will those live who live in thy Day? Will they resume this present form?"

The presupposition of these questions was invariably that an unqualified continuity existed between the mortal and the resurrected body. This continuity was of the same character as the continuity presupposed between the embodied and disembodied soul in the doctrine of immortality. The one as the doctrine of resuscitation and the other as the doctrine of immortality were no different in principle. In the one the continuity pertained to the whole man, in the other to a part of man. The fact that the one was typically Pharisaic and the other typically Platonic did not contradict the fact that they were essentially the same. The differences that distinguished them did not deny their common presupposition that man in whole or in part was in direct continuity through death with the beyond, however the latter was conceived. Both the resuscitation of the body and the immortality of the soul, as these define the hope of man, are forms of the infinite extension of man as he is, or of his *status quo*.

It is this presupposition which Paul, in a series of analogies from natural life, aims to correct (I Cor. 15:36-41). His sharp exclamatory remark: "You foolish man! What you sow does not come to life unless it dies" is an assertion of a fundamental discontinuity. It is not invalidated by his ancient conception of the biology of growth, in which the seed was presumed to have died before the plant came to life. Modern conceptions of continuity between the dormant life of the seed and the active life of the plant do not deny the change of form and the emergence of unpredictable differences. If the body involved in death provides us with no indication of how its resurrection is possible, the answer, according to Paul, is to be found in an action of God no stranger than emergent differences by which he gives a new body appropriate to the new order of existence. If the analogy suggests that "there are more things in heaven and earth . . . than are dreamt of in your philosophy [science] " (Shakespeare), at least the mind will be open to the possibility of an eventuality as strange as the resurrection of the body. This, as already indicated, will not be inconsistent with the strangeness of the natural world in which we live. Paul is explicit in his declaration that God gives the seed " a body as he has chosen, and to each kind of seed its own body " (v. 38). This means that God gives in relation both to the secret purpose of existence and to the immediate function served. Since the bodily differences of men, animals, birds, and fish, as well as those of the heavenly bodies — the sun, moon, and stars — are to be understood in this twofold manner, so are the differences of the resurrection body.

These differences are indicated in a series of contrasts which follow: "What is sown is perishable, what is raised is imperishable. It is sown in dishonor, it is raised in glory. It is sown in weakness, it is raised in power. It is sown a physical body, it is raised a spiritual body " (vs. 42-44). Since the question of the adequacy of the category " physical-spiritual " will be considered later, the main point at the moment is to recognize the discontinuity between what is sown and what is raised — on the one side what is perishable, dishonorable, and physical, and on the other side what is imperishable, glorious, and spiritual. The discontinuity derives from Paul's conception of the two ages — the one represented by the first Adam, in whom all die, the other, by the second Adam (Christ), in whom all shall be made alive (v. 22). There is a definite break between the two orders of existence. " As was the man of dust, so are those who are of the dust; and as is the man of heaven, so are those who are of heaven. Just as we have borne the image of the man of dust, we shall also bear the image of the man of heaven " (vs. 48-49).

This clarifies the statement that flesh and blood cannot inherit the Kingdom of God. It has no reference to the Greek and gnostic conception that the body in contrast to the soul is corrupt and perishable and therefore cannot inherit the Kingdom, whereas the soul can inherit it. It has reference only to the discontinuity between the old Adam and the new Adam, between that order of existence under the judgment which sin brought upon it and that characterized by resurrection as justification by grace (Rom. 5:12, 17; cf. Rom. 5:15). Flesh and blood would not refer, therefore, to the physical as such but to the whole man as a corporate member of the old Adam. Consequently, it would be less confusing to speak of a sinful, death-conditioned body that was sown than of a physical, or natural, body.

The decisive consideration at this point is Paul's conception of the transformation by which the discontinuity is overcome. This concerns the way in which it is overcome not only in the resurrection but in the changing of those who are alive at the coming of Christ and do not die as the majority of men (I Cor. 15:51-52). "Lo! I tell you a mystery," says Paul. "We shall not all sleep, but we shall all be changed, in a moment, in the twinkling of an eye, at the last trumpet. For the trumpet will sound, and the dead will be raised imperishable, and we shall be changed." The transformation as he describes it concerns this perishable nature putting on the imperishable, this mortal putting on immortality as a cloak over the whole man (v. 53).

But what does this mean? What precisely does Paul have in mind when he speaks of the change, or transformation, in this manner? Leaving aside his apocalyptic imagery of the trumpet's sounding to awaken the dead and summon the living, we recognize, first, that such a change, or transformation, represented by the metaphor of being clothed or invested with immortality, was not uncommon in his day. This should not occasion surprise, because even those who conceived of resurrection as resuscitation were not so naïve as to ignore the point of those who found difficulty in understanding what manner of body the resurrected dead would have. The rational and the speculative would compel some modification of a view that was too literal in its interpretation. Thus the Apocalypse of Baruch, in an extended section on the nature of the resurrection body, recognizes a transformation that resembles that of Paul except in two important respects. First, the dead are not raised, as Paul understands the event, but resuscitated, and following this, transformed as a result of divine judgment, the wicked becoming worse and the righteous better. Second, the transformation of the righteous is a reward based on justification by works (chs. 49 to 51).

The general connotation of such antithetical terms as " perishable " and " imperishable," " mortality " and " immortality," may obscure the fact that what Paul means by the transformation is the change from that order of existence represented by Adam to.that represented by Christ (ch. 15:22, 48). Since being in Adam means the bearing of his image, and being in Christ the bearing of his image, the transformation consists in the change from the one image to the other, but without a change in the essential identity of the person. For the latter to occur, would be tantamount to his destruction and contrary to the meaning of salvation. The evangelical nature of the transformation is indicated in the letter to the Romans, where it is stated that those whom God " foreknew he also predestined to be conformed to the image of his Son, in order that he might be the first-born among many brethren. And those whom he predestined, he also called; and those whom he called he also justified; and those whom he justified he also glorified " (Rom. 8:29-30). The transformation at the end, which is here described as glorification, is in sequence with justification, election, and predestination (cf. I Cor. 15:43; Rom. 8:18), and is therefore essentially evangelical.

The same conformation to the image of Christ is the predominant theme of the letter to the Philippians, where in ch. 3 Paul counts his former religious confidences as refuse that he might gain Christ. In his desire to become like Christ in his death (v. 10) his one persistent hope is that of attaining to the resurrection of the dead. Since he has not yet attained it, and for this reason is imperfect (immature), he presses forward like a runner toward the finish line to win this prize of the upward call of God in Christ (vs. 13-14). The prize is undoubtedly the resurrection of the body, which he specifies at the end of the chapter: " We await a Savior, the Lord Jesus Christ, who will change our lowly body to be like his glorious body, by the power which enables him even to subject all things to himself " (vs. 20-21). As the end stage of what began with Paul's acceptance of Christ as Lord and with the substitution of the gift of salvation for self-salvation (v. 9), the change is undoubtedly an evangelical transformation. Moreover, in this chapter, with its focus on the resurrection, Paul is influenced by his exhortation in the previous chapter that the Philippians should have the mind of Christ, " who, though he was in the form of God, . . . emptied himself, taking the form of a servant. . . . And being found in human form he humbled himself and became obedient unto death, even death on a cross " (ch. 2:6-8).

In these passages, and particularly in the identification with which Paul epitomizes faith as being crucified and raised with Christ, we have an indication of what he meant by the transformation at the end of a sinful, death-conditioned body into one that was spiritual. It was essentially the objective working out of the forgiveness of sins to its eschatological conclusion in the resurrection. If this were not so, and the resurrection were identified with the immortality of the soul or the resuscitation of the body, it would mean an extension of man in whole or in part as he is, without the forgiveness of sins.

Although, as in the Apocalypse of Baruch and other sources, the resurrection could be regarded as exclusively judgmental, this would not be the same eschatological conclusion as the one that follows from the forgiveness of sins through Christ. It is true, of course, according to Paul, that everyone must appear before the judgment seat of Christ (e.g., II Cor. 5:10), but for the believer the judgment is past in that he knows Christ no longer as a judge but as one who intercedes on his behalf. His confidence is that the forgiveness that has sustained him in life will issue in the resurrection of his body in its ultimate and glorious form. The transformation thus effected pertains to what is essentially personal, and this as inclusive of the body as it is commonly understood. It is the personal, inclusive of the bodily, now adapted to a new order of existence and freed from the conditions that sin and death impose, and therefore one in which the agape of God is fully realized. For this reason the transformation is wrongly understood if we conceive of it as from a physical to a spiritual body, in which the latter by definition is less and less of the former.

The objectification of forgiveness, not only in the reconciliation of the believer to God through Christ, but in the bodily resurrection of the believer, is only a way of saying that the Easter hope is integral to the gospel. Even in the forgiveness which one man is able to offer another, it is a mark of genuineness when the one who seeks forgiveness does everything humanly possible to rectify the wrong he has done. In the case of Zacchaeus, the publican, for example, when he accepted the forgiveness of God and sought it of those he had wronged, his first action was to declare, " Behold, Lord, the half of my goods I give to the poor; and if I have defrauded any one of anything, I restore it fourfold " (Luke 19:8). Such objectification of forgiveness on the part of a man is further exemplified in the Roman Catholic conception of doing penance. When penance is not a legalistic prescription but arises out of the heart in an honest effort to restore even more than was taken and thus to go beyond the strict limits of justice, it is essentially evangelical.

But the possibility of humanly rectifying what Paul means by guilt and death, as well as the futility to which existence is thereby subjected, is beyond us. Under these circumstances it is no longer possible for the one seeking forgiveness to make restitution. Instead, the seemingly impossible happens, namely, that the one wronged — the God of agape against whom the whole complex of darkness and of the wickedness of men is arrayed — makes restitution in Christ. He not only reconciles the heart of man to himself but fulfills the reconciliation in the eschatological objectification of forgiveness, which is the resurrection of the dead. In a word, the whole range of divine forgiveness, including the resurrection, is a manifestation of grace.

Paul now breaks forth into one of his great expressions of praise — a victory song of triumph over death, prompted by his realization that in the end the doom pronounced upon the world (Gen. 3:19) is removed and the triumph of Christ is absolute and everlasting. God is sovereign over all. " Then shall come to pass the saying that is written: ' Death is swallowed up in victory.' ' O death, where is thy victory? O death, where is thy sting? ' The sting of death is sin, and the power of sin is the law. But thanks be to God, who gives us the victory through our Lord Jesus Christ." (I Cor: 15:54-57.)

This is the language and the victory that provide the answer to all expressions of genuine sorrow, including the deep pathos of life as men wonder about themselves, puzzled to know who they are, whence they have come, and whither they are going. It is the answer not only to the enigmatic finality of bereavement, which is contradictory to the highest form of love and to the validity of the personal, but to the juggernaut of time and its power to nullify into oblivion the best achievements of men. If the loneliness of the individual is profoundly intensified not only in a world of enormous populations but in a universe of enormous proportions, it is even more intensified in an existence in which there is no way out of guilt and death. If, for him, as for millions like him, nothing essentially matters, what matters the world and the universe, for all their size? It is understandable, therefore, that the language of Paul and the victory he acclaims should provide the answer to the ancient writer whose insights are so representative of the disillusionment of the modern world with respect not only to cultural values but to any other reaction to the disillusionment except that of violence: " Then I saw that wisdom excels folly as light excels darkness. . . . Yet I perceived that one fate comes to all of them. Then I said to myself, ' What befalls the fool will befall me also; why then have I been so very wise? ' . . . How the wise man dies just like the fool!

So I hated life, because what is done under the sun was griev-
ous to me; for all is vanity and a striving after wind " (Eccl.
2:13-17).

But such despair of violence, which generates a perverted
confidence in action as a defense against emptiness (Eccl.
1:2-3; 2:1-17), and which has waited without anything happening or counting and has wearied of words and even of
thinking until it resorts to revolution, has not taken stock of
the deadness to which it reacts either within the world or
within itself. It is deadness of spirit — a strange condition that
comes over a man, making him hard of heart, indifferent to
feeling, slothful or apathetic, irresponsibly superficial or glib,
callously ambitious, enslaved to busyness, and if the occasion
demands it, savagely destructive. It is a deadness within, which,
from such a description, is a source of the greatest variety of
sin. Through such sin it destroys a man, just as a venomous
serpent poisons him (I Cor. 15:56). As such it is indicative of
a profound need of forgiveness which is comprehensive of
the whole man. The victory that Paul acclaims is a victory
over such deadness in nature as in man, in the world order as
in the individual. The victory is not merely figurative, subjective, or theoretical, but pertains to the whole of everyday
life and to the objective, historical world. It pertains to that
reality which will eclipse all that we presently know as reality and which will reveal it to have been deceptive. As the
assurance that nothing can separate us from the love of God
in Christ, not even death (Rom. 8:39), as the secret by which
the old has passed away and the new come (II Cor. 5:17),
it is the greatest source of joy (cf. Phil. 4:4). Thus, Paul can
exclaim with the profoundest gratitude, " Thanks be to God,
who gives us the victory through our Lord Jesus Christ "
(I Cor. 15:57; cf. Rom. 7:24-25). As the motivational source
of the ethical, such gratitude makes it inevitable that Paul
should add, " Therefore, my beloved brethren, be steadfast,
immovable, always abounding in the work of the Lord, knowing that in the Lord your labor is not in vain " (I Cor. 15:58).

REFERENCES AND NOTES

1. Henry Link, *Return to Religion* (The Macmillan Company, 1941), p. 55.

2. Jean Hering, *First Epistle of Paul to the Cornithians* (The Epworth Press, Publishers, London, 1962), p. 7.

3. Johannes Munck, *Paul and the Salvation of Mankind*, tr. by Frank Clarke (SCM Press Ltd., London, 1959 E.T.), p. 152.

4. Reinhold Niebuhr, *Beyond Tragedy* (Charles Scribner's Sons, 1937), Ch. 10: "Transvaluation of Values," sermonic essay on I Cor. 1:26-29.

5. T. S. Eliot. Compare his poem "Hollow Men."

6. Friedrich Nietzsche, *The Antichrist* (G. T. Foulis & Co., Ltd., London, 1911), pp. 127–231.

7. Karl Barth, *The Resurrection of the Dead* (Hodder & Stoughton, Ltd., London, 1933 E.T.), pp. 28–29.

8. Augustus M. Toplady. "Rock of Ages, Cleft for Me," verse 3, lines 1 and 2.

9. David Cox, *Jung and St. Paul* (Longmans, Green & Co., Inc., 1959), Ch. 2.

10. Jean-Paul Sartre, *No Exit*. Published under the title of "In Camera" in *Three European Plays* (Penguin Books, London, 1958).

11. J. Stanley Glen, *The Recovery of the Teaching Ministry* (The Westminster Press, 1960), pp. 99–102.

12. Carl R. Rogers, *Client-centered Therapy* (Houghton Mifflin Company, 1951).

13. Philip Mairet, ed., *Christian Essays in Psychiatry* (SCM Press Ltd., London, 1956). See "Individual Psychology," pp. 127–146.

14. James R. Moffatt, *First Epistle of Paul to the Corinthians* (Hodder & Stoughton, Ltd., London, 1947), p. 43.

15. Martin Luther, *Commentary on St. Paul's Epistle to the Galatians* (Fleming H. Revell Company, 1953), p. 59.

16. Adolf Deissmann, *Light from the Ancient East* (Harper & Brothers, New York, 1927 E.T.), pp. 301–303.

17. Hans Jonas, *The Gnostic Religion* (Beacon Press, Inc., 1958), pp. 270–281.

18. Frank Leslie Cross, ed. and tr., *The Jung Codex* (A. R. Mowbray & Company, London, 1955), pp. 13–34; Robert M. Grant, *Gnosticism and Early Christianity* (Columbia University Press, 1959), pp. 8–13; Hans Jonas, *op. cit.*

19. Karl Barth, *Church Dogmatics* (T. & T. Clark, Edinburgh, 1958), Vol. IV, Part II, pp. 736–746.

20. Derrick Sherwin Bailey, *The Mystery of Love and Marriage* (Harper & Brothers, 1952). Otto Piper, *The Biblical View of Sex and Marriage* (Charles Scribner's Sons, 1960).

21. Matthew Black, *The Scrolls and Christian Origins* (Charles Scribner's Sons, 1961).

22. Samuel Angus, *The Mystery-Religions and Christianity* (Charles Scribner's Sons, 1925), p. 216.

23. Sidney Cave, *The Christian Way* (Philosophical Library, Inc., 1955), pp. 183–184.

24. William E. H. Lecky, *History of European Morals* (Longmans, Green & Co., Ltd., London, 1920), p. 322.

25. Karl Menninger, *Love Against Hate* (Harcourt, Brace & Co., 1942), p. 53.

26. Hans Lietzmann, *Beginnings of the Christian Church* (Charles Scribner's Sons, 1949), p. 139.

27. James Moffatt, *op. cit.*, pp. 102, 140–141.

28. Rudolf Bultmann, *Gnosis*, Vol. V, in Gerhard Kittel, ed., *Bible Key Words*, tr. and ed. by J. R. Coates (A. & C. Black, Ltd., London, 1952). Robert M. Grant, *Gnosticism and Early Christianity* (Columbia University Press, 1950), p. 10.

29. William W. Sargant, *Battle for the Mind* (William Heinemann, Ltd., London, 1957), p. 223, quoted from Aldous Huxley, *The Devils of Loudun* (Chatto & Windus, London, 1952).

30. Jean Hering, *op. cit.*, p. 68.

31. C. F. D. Moule, " The Judgment Theme in the Sacraments," in *The Background of the New Testament and Its Eschatology*,

ed. by W. D. Davies, and D. Daube, in honor of C. H. Dodd (Cambridge University Press, 1956), pp. 464–481.

32. John Calvin, *Institutes of the Christian Religion*, ed. by John T. McNeill (The Westminster Press, Library of Christian Classics, 1960), IV. xiv. 19. See comment by J. Stalker on this aspect of Calvin's view of the sacraments, in Hastings, *Dictionary of Religion and Ethics* (T. & T. Clark, Edinburgh, 1925), Vol. X, p. 913. Although the Chrysostom source (*To Neophytes*) is omitted by later editors (e.g., Migne), it is recognized in Johannes Quasten, *Patrology* (The Newman Press, 1960), Vol. III, p. 452, on the basis of more recently discovered source material (1955). See Eduard Schweitzer, *Lordship and Discipleship* (SCM Press Ltd., London, 1960), p. 21, footnote 2.

33. W. D. Davies, *St. Paul and Rabbinical Judaism* (S.P.C.K., London, 1948), Ch. 9: "The Old and the New Obedience": II "The Death of Jesus."

34. Ecclesiasticus 25:4 (ca. 180 B.C.; Greek version, ca. 132 B.C.).

35. Philo Judaeus (Bohn, 1885), IV, 306.

36. Louis Ginzberg, *The Legends of the Jew* (Jewish Publication Society of America, 1901), I, 49–102. *Jewish Encyclopaedia* (Funk & Wagnalls Company, 1906), V, 332–335; S. Mathews, *New Testament Times in Palestine*, rev. ed. (The Macmillan Company, 1933), pp. 190–194; William O. E. Oesterley, and George H. Box. *Religion and Worship of the Synagogue* (Pittman & Sons, Bath, 1907), pp. 297–302; Frederick Robert Tennant, *The Sources of the Doctrines of the Fall and Original Sin* (Cambridge University Press, 1903), Chs. 5–7.

37. John Calvin, *Commentary on First Corinthians* (Wm. B. Eerdmann's Publishing Company, 1948), pp. 353–354.

38. D. M. MacKinnon, "Sacrament and Common Meal," in D. E. Nineham, ed., *Studies in the Gospels* (Basil Blackwell & Mott, Ltd., Oxford, 1955), pp. 201–207.

39. Oscar Cullmann, "Meaning of the Lord's Supper in Primitive Christianity," in Oscar Cullmann and F. J. Leenhardt, *Essays on the Lord's Supper* (John Knox Press, 1959), pp. 5–23.

40. Joachim Jeremias, *The Eucharistic Words of Jesus* (Basil Blackwell & Mott, Ltd., Oxford, 1955), pp. 159–165. Douglas Jones, *Anamnēsis* in the LXX and the Interpretation of I Cor. 11:25, *Journal of Theological Studies*, 6, 1955, pp. 183–191.

41. Thus differing from C. F. D. Moule, *loc. cit.*

42. Norman Snaith, *The Distinctive Ideas of the Old Testament* (The Westminster Press, 1946), Ch. 5, " The Covenant-Love of God."

43. Joachim Jeremias, *The Parables of Jesus* (Charles Scribner's Sons, 1955).

44. See J. Stanley Glen, *op. cit.*, Ch. 1: " Subordination of the Teaching Ministry."

45. Eduard Schweitzer, *et al.*, *Spirit of God*, in *Kittel's Bible Key Words*, Vol. III (A. & C. Black, Ltd., London, 1960), p. 67.

46. *Ibid.*, p. 64.

47. Paul S. Minear, *Images of the Church in the New Testament* (The Westminster Press, 1960), pp. 193-194.

48. Joseph Haroutunian, *How to Hear the Gospel* (Centenary Address, Knox College, Toronto, 1958), pp. 9-10.

49. Walther Eichrodt, *Theology of the Old Testament*, Vol. I, tr. by J. A. Baker (The Westminster Press, The Old Testament Library, 1961), p. 251.

50. Hans Lietzmann, *An die Korinther I–II* (Mohr, Tübingen, 1931), p. 62.

51. Frederick Dillistone, " How Is the Church Christ's Body? " (*Theology Today*, 11, 1945), pp. 56–58.

52. H. Wheeler Robinson, " Hebrew Psychology," in *The People and the Book*, ed. by A. S. Peake, pp. 353–382. Aubrey R. Johnson, *The One and the Many in the Israelite Conception of God* (University of Wales Press, Cardiff, 1961).

53. Walther Eichrodt, *Man in the Old Testament* (SCM Press Ltd., London, 1951), Ch. 3: " The Antinomies of the Unconditional Ought."

54. *Ibid.*, p. 42.

55. D. G. Delling, *Worship in the New Testament* (Darton, Longman & Todd, Ltd., London, 1962), footnote, p. 177. It would be compromised by the view here represented.

56. Johannes Pedersen, *Israel: Its Life and Culture*, Vols. I, II (Geoffrey Cumberlege, Oxford University Press, London, E.T. 1946), pp. 308–310.

57. Karl Barth, *Church Dogmatics:* " Agape-love takes place in affinity, eros-love in opposition, to human nature," Vol. IV, Part 2, p. 743.

58. Karen Horney, *The Neurotic Personality of Our Time* (W. W. Norton & Company, Inc., 1937): " A child can stand a

great deal of what is often regarded as traumatic — as long as he feels wanted and loved," p. 80. Rollo May, *The Meaning of Anxiety* (The Ronald Press Co., 1950): "Not being loved is better than the experience of pseudo love for a child," p. 343.

59. Karl Barth, *Church Dogmatics*, Vol. IV, Part II, Sec. 68: "The Holy Spirit and Christian Love," pp. 727–840. Gottfried Quell and Ethelbert Stauffer, *Love*, in *Kittel's Bible Key Words*, Vol. I (A. & C. Black, Ltd., London, 1949).

60. Eduard Schweitzer, *et al.*, *op. cit.*, pp. 7, 66.

61. *Ibid.*, p. 80.

62. Walther Eichrodt, *Theology of the Old Testament*, pp. 318–319.

63. Martin Esslin, *The Theatre of the Absurd* (Anchor Book, Doubleday & Company, Inc., 1961), p. 298.

64. *Ibid.*, p. 43.

65. Karl Barth, *The Resurrection of the Dead*, p. 148.

66. The perfect tense, *egēgertai*, indicates that for Paul it is not an isolated event: vs. 12, 13, 14, 17.

67. Oscar Cullmann, *Immortality of the Soul or Resurrection of the Dead* (The Epworth Press, Publishers, London, 1958).

68. William Macneile Dixon, *The Human Situation* (Galaxy Book, Gifford Lectures, 1935–1937, Oxford University Press, 1958), p. 237.

69. Karl Barth, *The Resurrection of the Dead*, p. 177.

70. *Ibid.*, pp. 177–178.

71. Jean Hering, *op. cit.*, pp. 164–169.